# FIERCE LOYALTY®

The high impact leadership formula
to transform employee engagement

## LOUISE MALLAM

# Praise for *FIERCE Loyalty*®

"In today's volatile business environment, cultivating loyal employees is more important than ever. Louise Mallam's book is full of wise advice and practical strategies for building loyal, motivated and outstanding teams."

**Marshall Goldsmith,** executive coach, business educator and New York Times-bestselling author, ranked the number one leadership thinker in the world by Thinkers50

•••

"Highly engaging and practical approach on how to lead with impact, making you want to turn every page. Louise draws on her professional and personal experiences, which makes FIERCE Loyalty® a real pleasure to read. Make sure you get a hard copy as you'll want to highlight, make notes and refer back to a great deal of the material. A must read for every leader."

**Nousheh Paris,** Sales Director, American Express

•••

"Louise understands that the lifeblood of any successful organization is its employee's engagement with their leaders, the company vision and the fun journey that accompanies these things. *FIERCE Loyalty*® is cohesive and clear in building a model that supports employees at all levels who can contribute, feel valued as people and behave as leaders in any role. Employee engagement is not something to be 'driven' to success, it is a combination of things that anyone can get right by following Louise's easy to implement model. This book will help any leader transform themselves, their team and their organization into a force to be reckoned with. An insightful and exciting must read that I can see being adopted globally and successfully."

**Leo Muckley,** Team Manager, Amazon

•••

"I started reading *FIERCE Loyalty*® feeling quite skeptical and thinking 'another one of those books telling me how to do my job and how people behave'. But this is a must read for anyone who cares about employees and cares about what matters to them and written by a real professional in real terms. I couldn't put it down, nodding fiercely in agreement with the observations and analysis found. I will be implementing a lot of the findings and sharing with key stakeholders as it takes the value of engagement and smacks you in the face with it! Valuable, well written and practical for modern businesses in an age where we should be keeping, not mistreating, employee loyalty."

**Kathryn Chambers,** HR Manager, Poupart

•••

"Take it from me, if you want to see big changes and create teams of people who want to work for you, then this is the book for you. Once you have been through this process there's no going back as you see how counter-productive your old ways of thinking and behaving were. Try it, absorb it, you won't regret it."

**Sarah Lewis,** Learning and Development Specialist

•••

"An enlightening and refreshing slant on the topic of engagement with a realistic focus. The down to earth wording allows you to embrace its message and make real changes. I will be recommending this read to my colleagues and HR peers."

**Sarah Singer,** Regional HR Manager, ENGIE

"A must read for any leader who is ambitious about creating an engaging environment where employees enjoy working. The book offers inspiring advice and practical examples that systematically lead to highly engaged and performing teams."

**Zuzana Olleova,** Head of HR Operations, Swiss Re

•••

"Engagement is a buzzword in organisations these days with very little practical advice on how to achieve it. Louise's model throws light on how to approach engagement in a way that works and persists over time."

**Christian Riedhammer,** Team Manager, Amazon

•••

"Anyone who ever wanted to crack the engagement puzzle in their team or organisation can benefit from the down to earth knowledge in this book."

**Alex McColl,** EU Learning and Performance Manager, Amazon

# RETHINK PRESS

For Brigid, for inspiring the leader in me

and helping me to love Mondays

# CONTENTS

# FOREWORD

There are so many skills that a successful leader needs to master and balance, so how do you choose which to focus on? The absence of any creates a vacuum that could spell disaster. Over-indexing on one usually leads to under-representation in another. And when and how each skill is applied is subject to ever-changing forces and conditions.

It's hard being a leader!

There are the skills of leading the business: seeing and taking advantage of market trends; setting business strategy and steering an effective course to get there; financial control and management; and so on. Then there are the people leadership skills: motivation, influencing, team cohesion and performance, and delivering difficult messages. And then there are the skills of self-leadership: emotional intelligence, personal development, awareness of bias towards others and correcting one's behaviours.

No leader masters them all; it's a journey. Some are blessed with natural skill in some areas and a devotion to improvement in the others. I've spent a significant part of my leadership career becoming the very best leader I could; I'm still on that journey. On my way, I've come to the firm conviction that businesses are first and foremost their people - staff, customers, leaders, contractors and suppliers - and that how leaders treat the people in the organisation is the critical success factor. The primary indicator of this is employee engagement.

In *FIERCE Loyalty®* you will step through the reasons for disengagement, the financial cost - which is astonishingly high - and the business impact. Through the FIERCE Loyalty® model you will get the tools, skills and knowledge to become a leader of highly engaged teams. In doing so, you will not only create a vibrant and stimulating place to work, you will drive business results, improve the customer experience and stand out as an employer of choice. Last, but not least, you yourself will become a better leader!

So aim high, and remember: it's OK to love Mondays.

**Andreas von der Heydt**
Director at Kindle, Amazon, LinkedIn influencer, author of *The 7 Qualities of Tomorrow's Top Leaders*

# INTRODUCTION

## Who is this book for?

Although all leaders could benefit from this book, it's specifically written for senior leaders in large organisations where there is a greater distance (levels and numbers) between them and the shop floor, making it harder for them to have their finger on the pulse.

The book doesn't focus on the strategic planning element, which is where senior leaders come into their own. Although that may seem counter-intuitive, there are two reasons for it.

**In my experience, senior leaders know how to create strategy.** They need no instruction. What they lack is the why - 'Why should I focus on engagement?' Once they have the why front of mind, e.g. the financial and business data, they are well-equipped to form a strategy.

**Engagement is happening in the minute by minute experiences of the workforce.** Strategy is of course the starting point, but it's the downstream operational practices and implementation that have the biggest impact on engagement.

If you're thinking, *This is a useful book and model for my reports, but not for me at my level,* that thinking is part of the engagement problem in your organisation.

Engagement filters down, not up. People replicate what they consistently see their leaders doing (i.e. the organisation's culture). This happens throughout the entire organisation, right to the very top. Your day to day example is what your reports are replicating, and what their reports are replicating, and so on. If you have a well-prepared engagement strategy, but the entire senior leadership team isn't standing firmly behind it by their consistent actions, it will never be implemented properly. People are hardwired to follow and copy what you do, not what you say you will do in a strategy document.

When senior leaders actively embrace the FIERCE Loyalty® model with their reports, they in turn cascade the process throughout the organisation, creating an irresistible force that ultimately becomes the culture.

It must start with you. It cannot start at middle management; it must flow down from senior leaders. The examples used in this book cover senior directors to front line supervisors. Their drivers and needs are the same, regardless of who they report to. By all means share the book with others, but you yourself must digest it first of all and be the example.

This book is for you if you want:

- Happy, productive, engaged and fiercely loyal teams
- To see those teams and the individuals within them grow, thrive and become superstars
- Better business results
- The legend of your organisation's employee engagement to be so vibrant that top talent seeks you out
- Happier customers
- Productivity and effectiveness to self-regulate, allowing you to lead, not manage

O To stop having conversations about attitude, lateness and inconsistent behaviour

O To look forward to Monday mornings.

This book is not for you if none of the above is appealing.

# Great leadership

There are many definitions of leadership. Here is mine:

> Great leaders inspire passion and deliver stellar results through the willing efforts of others.

Your job isn't to make things easy; it's to get people to want to join you on the journey, see their part in the bigger picture and feel good about themselves and their contribution.

If you've tried to resolve the engagement puzzle in your organisation before and it hasn't worked, don't try harder, try something different.

# EMPLOYEE ENGAGEMENT

There is a question that echoes around the walls of so many organisations today: 'Why are our people leaving?'

This is a question I have heard hundreds of times in dozens of organisations over the past twenty-five years, from global Goliaths like Amazon to UK-based utilities companies and banks. At the heart of it is the same issue – I've sat in so many post-mortem discussions where senior leaders want to discover why a key person has left, and why nobody knew they were intending to leave until it was too late.

But the question 'Why are our people leaving?' isn't the right question to ask. The question should be 'Why aren't our people engaged?' Attrition is just a downstream impact of poor engagement. And the focus on the people who leave the organisation isn't the right focus, because the group of people who stay is far larger and causes more damage to profits, service and reputation as they resist, underperform and undermine at every turn.

People don't want to do joyless, meaningless work for a leader who treats their employees like numbers and expects behaviour they themselves are unwilling to exhibit. The difference today is that they can easily do something about it: change jobs. But knowing that as a leader and doing something about it are two very different things (more on the knowing/doing gap later).

I believe all leaders truly want to solve the engagement puzzle for many reasons. First of all, who wouldn't want to work in a vibrant and stimulating workplace? And constantly re-hiring and retraining new staff is a headache for leaders. Then there is the lost tribal knowledge and positive attitude of those leaving, creating a talent and motivation drain. For the people who stay, morale is so low that they underperform and merely 'exist', if you can even call it that. In addition, as an organisation's reputation begins to suffer, it becomes harder to attract talent in the first place, so a vicious cycle ensues. It's frustrating and exhausting.

The problem is compounded by today's age of social media, where a new job is never more than a click away. Job mobility is rising as quickly as job loyalty is falling. Something must be done to stem the tide.

Typically, when leaders focus on driving engagement, they focus on things like salary, benefits, the office environment, posh coffee machines, etc. While those things are important, they're not what engage people when it comes to passion and purpose. They won't encourage those people to choose to elevate themselves and own their results.

When organisations measure the engagement issue, they usually have a good sense for the level of employee engagement (although a yearly survey is a poor tool). HR can provide up to date staff turnover stats, but what most organisations consistently fail to do is wrap an accurate financial price tag around the issue. If they did, the shock alone would kick-start them into a period of intense activity, focus and resource allocation until the hitherto unseen financial risk was under control.

So let's begin with the 'why'. Why should you even have this on your radar? Why is this one of the biggest hidden risks in most organisations? Why should precious time, resource and budget be allocated to measuring and addressing engagement? Basically, why read this book?

# The hidden cost of low engagement

The problem with disengaged employees is two-fold. Firstly, there's the group of people who are so disengaged that they leave. Then there is the second group, who may be just as disengaged, but they stay.

Let's begin with the people who leave.

The monetary cost of staff attrition accounts for recruitment costs, HR time, reduction in performance, training, temporary staff, other employees covering responsibilities, ramp time for the new starter, etc. **Oxford Economics** cited the annual attrition cost (UK) to five key sectors - Legal, Accountancy, IT/Tech, Media/Advertising and Retail - as £4.13bn in 2014. It cannot be ignored.

I have a high-level calculation to start the conversation with business leaders, and a detailed calculator based on an organisation's specific data. The figures for both are conservative. For some of the larger organisations I've consulted with, the cost of losing staff has been tens of millions of pounds per annum. For the high-level calculation, I divide this between leader and non-leader leavers.

For non-leader leavers, I apply a figure of £30,000 per person (based on Oxford Economics' 2014 quoted figure of £30,614 per person, which factors in twenty-eight weeks for the new person to become effective and logistical costs such as interviewing, advertising, etc.). Put simply, if you lost ten people last year in non-leadership roles, it cost your business £300,000; if you lost one hundred people, it cost you £3million.

I typically work with organisations that employ 10,000+ employees and have an attrition rate of greater than 20% (some are nearly 50%). An organisation with 10,000 employees predicting it will lose

2,000 people on the figures cited above would lose £60million. That's worth repeating...£60million.

You'll never stop attrition altogether, nor would you want to. There are benefits to staff movement, and some people leave for reasons other than engagement. But if we could prevent even 25% of leavers from exiting the business, using the stats above we'd save £15million. This is why we start with 'why'.

For leadership level leavers it's standard practice to apply a multiple of salary depending on seniority within the organisation. It usually takes longer to hire a new leader, longer to ramp, and the span of influence and impact of the outgoing person is wider. This figure can be as high as 250% of salary for senior executives To be conservative and provide a mid-point for examples prior to the detailed calculation, I apply 120% of salary. Using this calculation, I predict the cost of losing someone on £60,000 pa is £72,000 to the business. How many leaders have you lost in the past year? If you lost ten people on this salary, it cost your business £720,000, and if you lost one hundred people, it cost your business £7.2million.

If you're curious about the detailed calculator, visit www.LeadingEdgePerformance.org/calculator

The reason the financial cost of staff turnover isn't front of mind for many organisations is because mostly it's intangible. While there is a visible cost for advertising the role and some other parts of the hiring process, nobody signs a cheque or settles an invoice for lost knowledge, or motivation drain, or interview time, or ramp time, or the time a position can be vacant, or lost productivity of those who cover work, or the ripple effect it can have through teams, and so on. To quote a favourite, albeit old, saying: 'If you can't measure it, you can't manage it'.

Usually, once I've highlighted the financial cost and risk of people leaving to senior leaders, the conversation and strategic plans quickly move on. But there is an additional risk and cost that's worth tabling.

It's more challenging to measure, and in my opinion vastly more dangerous to organisations: the disengaged people who stay.

They're unhappy, but not active enough to look elsewhere. Instead, they cause incalculable damage as they resist, resent, undermine, underperform. They need to be managed rather than led as they fail to self-manage even the most basic tasks, such as good attendance. Change is a bitterly contested notion. Relationship tension causes unnecessary conflict. Customer service levels are low and erode brand reputation.

That may sound extreme, but it's happening in many organisations today.

# Driving employee engagement

In addition to the costs saved by reducing staff turnover, driving employee engagement has numerous business benefits.

The financial implications of the disengaged remainers are staggering. According to a **Gallup** report, based on thirty years of research with over 30 million employees:

*Work units in the top quartile in employee engagement outperformed bottom-quartile units by 10% on customer ratings, 22% in profitability, and 21% in productivity. Work units in the top quartile also saw significantly lower turnover (25% in high-turnover organizations, 65% in low-turnover organizations), shrinkage (28%), and absenteeism (37%), and fewer safety incidents (48%), patient safety incidents (41%), and quality defects (41%).*

GALLUP'S 2016 Q12 META-ANALYSIS – THE NINTH THAT GALLUP HAS CONDUCTED SINCE 1997 – EXAMINES THE EFFECT OF EMPLOYEE ENGAGEMENT ON ORGANISATIONS' BOTTOM LINE.

The research goes on to add that companies with highly engaged workforces outperform their peers by **147%** in earnings per share. Another shocking statistic it reports is that **87%** of employees are disengaged at work.

The good news is that for the majority of people in this camp, the situation can be turned around. There are only six key steps any leader needs to master to fully engage the people they lead. And for the few inevitable remaining resisters, there's always the door.

There are of course employees who rock. They choose to have good attitudes, regardless of external factors, and operate at high levels. They are self-led, delighting in giving everyone they contact a stellar experience, and they understand the changing nature of businesses, and thrive in it. They too are out there, they're just not the focus of this book.

---

*There are organisations with such high levels of employee engagement that top talent seeks them out. Employees are fiercely loyal, operating at very high levels in self-directed ways, and customer service levels are legend. These people are set apart by a love of Mondays.*

---

# Plasters don't work

I've always been fascinated by the link between overall engagement levels and leadership styles in an organisation. Engagement filters down, not up. Some leaders just 'get it'; sadly, most don't. But, as a great teacher once told me, if it's possible for someone, it's possible for anyone.

I've spent many years learning from the role model leaders I've been blessed to know, sharpening my knowledge of the subject as a leadership development expert and honing my own leadership skill. What I've discovered is presented to you in this book.

Most organisations look to put a 'plaster' over the engagement problem, when what they really need is a fundamental change in the culture, starting with senior leaders. The aim of the culture shift is threefold:

1.  Retain talent - stop good people from leaving

2.  Improve performance and results - drive engagement so high that 'talent' becomes the norm in the organisation rather than the exception

3.  Improve morale - create a vibrant high-performance place to work in that people are fiercely loyal to and other talent wants to join.

# The Loyalty Advantage

Leaders and organisations that engage the workforce inspire loyalty, and those organisations win: fact.

It doesn't matter how great your products are, how fancy your marketing is, how shiny your offices are or how efficient you are at delivering to deadlines if underpinning your organisation is an ineffective, unproductive, disengaged, disloyal workforce ready to leap at the first opportunity that comes along. If you don't already have a highly engaged, fiercely loyal workforce, you're building on sand and your business is at risk.

However, if you get this piece of the puzzle right, you can almost sit back and watch the magic unfold as your creative and smart workforce shows you the levels of mastery they are capable of. It's breath-taking to watch.

---

*It doesn't make sense to hire smart people and then tell them what to do; we hire smart people so they can tell us what to do.*

**STEVE JOBS**

---

# The Promised Land

Allow me to paint a picture of what it would be like to have a highly engaged, fiercely loyal workforce.

Imagine work is a place you look forward to coming to, even on a Monday morning. You don't feel that dreaded knot of anxiety on a Sunday evening as you stare into another week at work; the joy doesn't drain out of you with the last few hours of the weekend. Both you and your team push up against the very edges of your capabilities and grow to heights you can barely imagine. You love to tell people where you work because you know what flashes through their mind when you do: wow, lucky you! You share knowing looks with colleagues when your teams are on fire with enthusiasm. Mistakes are rare, always unintentional, and those responsible own them and would walk over hot coals to rectify them. Customers are raving about your organisation because what you do rocks. People don't want to leave; they stay and thrive.

I've seen teams like this, I've been in teams like this, and I've led teams like this. It's a truly remarkable experience. And it's easier than you might think to achieve.

# The Quest

---

*If you could get all the people in an organization rowing*

*in the same direction, you could dominate any industry,*

*in any market, against any competition, at any time.*

**PATRICK LENCIONI**

---

When I work with organisations to drive engagement through the effectiveness of their leadership teams - the only place it can happen - I need to understand the direction they're heading in to help them to steer the course. I start by posing three key questions:

1. What kind of organisation are you trying to build?

2. What kind of teams do you want to lead?

3. How do you want your employees to feel about the organisation and their role?

These may be questions you've considered before. If not, go ahead and reflect on the answers for a few minutes. They're important.

The answers to question 1 are usually along the lines of:

○ Profitable, successful, growing consistently, etc.

○ Well respected brand, loyal customers, highest Net Promoter Score (NPS)

○ A great, fun place to work, high Glassdoor Employer results.

The answers to question 2 are usually along the lines of:

- High performing, effective, self-directed teams
- Engaged and self-motivated
- Capable of moving up when the opportunity arises.

The answers to question 3 are usually along the lines of:

- Loyal to the company; heads not turned by any and every other opportunity
- Proud to tell people where they work
- Enjoy work because they grow and thrive.

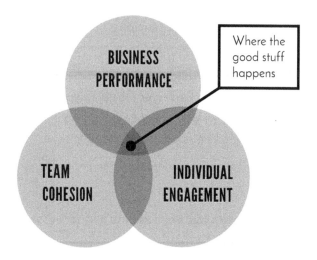

The answers above are fairly predictable, but in my experience so is something else: when I look at the organisation's current state compared to those aspirations, there is usually a wide, glaring gap. Leaders want these organisation, team and engagement levels, but are pretty far from the mark in delivering them. They're scratching their heads, wondering why, despite their best efforts, things don't work. Or perhaps they do for short periods, but they don't stick.

# Reverse engineering

If you are planning a journey to an unfamiliar destination, you may well use a satnav. The first thing you do is enter the precise destination, not some vague notion of it. With that clear destination in mind, the satnav can then reverse engineer the best route based on certain parameters, e.g. travelling via motorways, avoiding tolls, through a certain town, etc. It may have to reroute along the way, e.g. because of an unexpected traffic jam, but it will still get you to that precise point.

It's the same with the vision you have for your organisation and teams in terms of engagement: you've got to know where you're heading before you can plot the course.

So how will you know you've arrived at the desired destination? What would a fiercely loyal, highly engaged and effective workforce be like? In the immortal words of Stephen Covey, let's 'start with the end in mind'. Let's get a clear destination so that you and your teams can reverse engineer the best route, re-routing along the way if you need to.

Give this exercise the time it deserves and come back to it often. Remind yourself where you're heading and make improvements as the path becomes clearer. Involve your peers and teams.

---

*Any idea that is held in the mind, that is emphasized, that is either feared or revered, will begin at once to cloth itself in the most convenient and appropriate form available*

**ANDREW CARNEGIE**

---

# Start with the end in mind

The ability to hold your goal consistently and clearly on the screen of your mind gives you a business advantage.

First of all, choose a timescale, a checking in point. It doesn't mean that's when you'll be 100% there. In fact, once you get to 100%, you'll be able to see how much further you could go and set a new 100%. I recommend six–twelve months from now, but you know the challenge that lies ahead better than I. Choose a specific date, not just a month, or by the year end.

Now imagine it's the date you've chosen, and you've achieved your goal. What is the difference between then and now? What has changed? How do you know? What's the evidence?

To assist in bringing this to life, use the table below.

| TEAM IMPACT | | | |
|---|---|---|---|
| **WHAT WILL YOU SEE?** | **WHAT WILL YOU HEAR?** | **WHAT WILL YOU EXPERIENCE?** | **HOW WILL YOU FEEL?** |
| ▪ e.g. team members proactively supporting one another/ownership of issues | ▪ e.g. improved customer feedback/ NPS feedback/ proactive peer-support in team meetings | ▪ e.g. winning a team award/ Glassdoor Top 50 Companies to Work For | ▪ e.g. proud in the increase of internal promotions |
| BUSINESS IMPACT | | | |
| **WHAT WILL YOU SEE?** | **WHAT WILL YOU HEAR?** | **WHAT WILL YOU EXPERIENCE?** | **HOW WILL IT FEEL?** |
| ▪ e.g. inter-dept. collaboration/business goals collectively owned | ▪ e.g. unsolicited feedback across teams (given and received well) | ▪ e.g. attrition reduction to lowest level | ▪ e.g. creative and innovative |

| FINANCIAL MEASURES | | | |
| --- | --- | --- | --- |
| STAFF TURNOVER | ENGAGEMENT SCORES | PROMOTIONS/HIRES | OVERALL RESULTS |
| ▪ Decrease from ___% to ____% staff turnover rate resulting in a £_____ saving to the business | ▪ Increase of ___% in employee engagement survey results linked to a ___% increase in NPS score/customer satisfaction scores/ customer retention increase, etc. | ▪ Increase of ___% in internal promotions resulting in a £_____ saving in external hire costs<br>▪ Talent acquisition measures | ▪ Increase of ____%/£ _____ in sales/turnover/ profit, etc.<br>▪ Positive changes in the annual appraisal ratings from X to Y |

These are examples. Naturally, using your own business's specific measures or current pain-points is advisable.

Once you've mapped this out, I recommend you focus on just one specific team measure, business measure and financial measure. The rest are likely to follow naturally; they're all rivers running to the same sea, but the tactical plans can be more focused.

By choosing one goal from each layer, you are more likely to gain support from the entire senior leadership team for your efforts. Operations leaders will be keenly interested in a decreased staff turnover rate so the constant rehire process can end and experience can grow. Customer Service leaders will be very happy to support a project that increases NPS and the customer experience. HR leaders will be supportive of anything that reduces performance management issues and increases morale. Resourcing leaders will like the idea of being able to attract and place higher calibre candidates. Finance leaders will be delighted at the thought of saving millions of pounds per annum, and everyone up to the CEO will embrace a project that increase performance and business results. And let's not forget the employees themselves, including the leadership team, thriving in an engaging environment: the ultimate goal.

Everybody wins when you focus on engagement.

# The FIERCE Loyalty® Model

Now that you have the clear destination, the FIERCE Loyalty® model illuminates the route. There are only six key steps to master:

- **Focus On Yourself First** - if you can't lead yourself, you haven't earned the right to lead others

- **Inspire Self-belief** - build a solid foundation of trust and confidence so people feel they can succeed

- **Educate** - clarify what the leader expects and their definition of success

- **Raise The Bar** - introduce significant gear shifts that inspire passion and purpose so people want to succeed

- **Career Conversation** - willingly prepare people to move on (internally) so they succeed

- **Empower** - step back to allow self-direction where the employee teaches you about success.

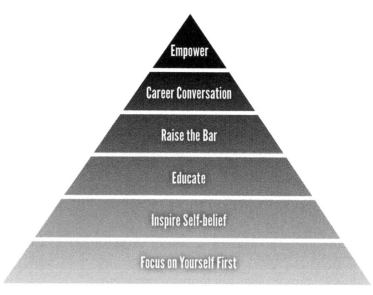

The six steps are simple and don't need to be over engineered, but each must be mastered in turn before you move on to the next. This is where most leaders go wrong: they jump around between the stages, or miss parts out. Instead of building a firm, solid structure, they build on sand.

We'll look at each stage in turn. As the visual indicates, the time you spend in each phase gets progressively shorter as employees become more and more engaged and present in the process.

There has never been a greater need for role model leaders who have such a positive influence that the effects radiate throughout people's lives, far beyond the work arena. I had such a leader twenty years ago. Brigid literally transformed my life – who I am, how I am, how I interact with others and the high standards I set for myself. Under her leadership I quickly became highly engaged, fiercely loyal to her and the organisation, operating at the very top of my game in mostly self-directed ways. But the true gift she gave me was to love Mondays. I couldn't wait to get in to work, even though I had a fantastic life out of work. It was such an engaging experience it didn't even feel like work.

But Brigid also gave me the most awful and devastating piece of feedback I have ever received; even now, twenty years later, the emotional impact it had on me still affects me. I'll share it with you in a later chapter. My point here is this: great leaders transforms lives. They don't make it easy; they make it compelling and possible. They leave positive footprints across the rest of your life as you reach levels you didn't even know existed.

It's impossible to predict how long this will take for you and your employees as it varies from person to person. It took approximately six months with Brigid and myself (she had already comfortably mastered the first phase, Focus On Yourself First, before we met). With my own reports, I have taken some people to the final stage in as little as three months.

Remember, you must master the stages, not just understand them. That bit is easy.

# Aware, care and dare

Special thanks to my colleague, **Debbie Ash**, for this neat phrase and thinking funnel, which I use often.

If you want to crack the engagement puzzle, you need to have three fundaments pieces in place:

**Aware** - you have to understand what's disengaging your workforce, know how big the risk is to your business, and acknowledge the part you are playing in the problem and the solution. This book is the gateway to awareness.

**Care** - you've got to care enough about the issue to be prepared to do something about it. Not your peers (although that certainly helps), not your team, but you. I know that probably sounds rather obvious, but you'd be surprised how many leaders I work with who happily kick their issues over the fence for me to solve for them. They aren't prepared to do the hard work or self-analysis needed to make any meaningful progress.

**Dare** - you need to face directly in to the issue, uncomfortable as it may be, and have the courage and resilience to alter course. What are you prepared to do/stop/give up to make this happen?

# Summary

○ Poor engagement cannot be ignored

○ If you don't already have a highly engaged, fiercely loyal workforce, you're building on sand

○ Don't ask, 'Why are our people leaving?', ask why they're not engaged

○ Think about the disengaged people who stay

○ Plasters won't work, they add to the problem

○ Engagement filters down, not up. The solution must start at the top

○ The good stuff happens at the inter-section of business performance, team cohesion and individual engagement

○ Have a clear vision and share it

○ Strategy is only effective when the entire senior leadership team stands behind it and demonstrates the behaviours necessary to get there.

# FOCUS ON YOURSELF FIRST

*When you were made a leader you weren't*
*given a crown, you were given the responsibility to*
*bring out the best in others.*

**JACK WELCH**

What if I told you that by mastering one important aspect of leadership, you would see dramatic improvements in engagement and results compared to where you are today? That there is an easy process to step through to engage and motivate others? That helping others to surface their own immense reservoirs of talent and creativity is not only easy, it is enjoyable, and leads to massive leaps in performance and results?

Maybe you've been in or led a team like this before, but you weren't exactly sure how it came about. Perhaps you know another leader who seems to lead exceptional teams and deliver stellar results effortlessly. What's their secret?

Well, it's no secret at all. In fact, the route to it is so simple and obvious that once you know it, you'll marvel at the fact that leaders like that are in the minority. They're so rare, in fact, that they stand out like bursts of light against the night sky.

Having been on both sides of the situation, being led like this and leading like this, I've made it my mission to share the way to do it with as many leaders as I can. It starts, as it must, by focusing on yourself.

# The Opportunity All Around You

In 2006 I moved to Koh Samui, Thailand and ran my own dive centre: Blue Planet. It was an incredible experience, and for two years I thrived in the sunshine and freedom of my lifestyle. The days were exceptionally long and the work was physical and demanding, but it was a joy.

For ten months of the year the business was busy, packed with happy divers and scuba students, and then the rainy season started. For two months there was no diving as the weather conditions were appalling. Even on a tropical island, it's pretty boring when you can't go anywhere without getting drenched.

I'm far too active to sit around waiting for rain to stop, so I had to occupy my mind. My attention soon turned to keeping up the modest amount of Spanish I had learned in South America the year before. The question was how would I do that in Thailand?

I played with the idea for a few days. Then, as I walked to work one day - the same route I had walked for the preceding ten months - I saw something fluttering in a shop window. On an A4 hand-written poster, the kind with tiny slivers of phone numbers hanging underneath, which had clearly been there for a while as it was pretty faded and crumpled, was an advert for Spanish lessons from a native speaker who lived on the island.

What a happy coincidence.

Well...not really. The poster, or rather the opportunity, had been there all along. I just hadn't been consciously aware of it. Like thousands of other bits of information constantly surrounding me but of no real perceived value, I had overlooked it for months. It had been in my conscious blindspot until it seemed useful to me.

As you read through the ideas in this book, you're likely to begin to see opportunities that have existed all around you for a long time: people you could speak to; processes you could improve; meetings that could be more effective; tasks you could delegate; star performers in the making; inter-departmental collaboration projects; external partners who hold the key.

And if you re-read the book, you'll probably see information you didn't digest before, and recognise qualities in yourself that weren't there before.

There are a lot of bad people leaders out there. But they are typically fantastic at leading the business. I should know - I've met, worked with, trained, coached, mentored and reported to hundreds of them over the years. Men, women, old and young, from CEOs to first time team leaders - the full spectrum. And I can safely say that role model people leaders are the exception. How sad. How dangerous.

I guess it's no real surprise. After all, humans learn most effectively by replicating what they consistently see, hear and experience (i.e. the culture). So if a person doesn't see, hear or experience truly great leadership, then it follows that they can't replicate it. I dread to think of the leader I would be today without Brigid's excellent example.

These important skills aren't to be learned from books or seminars, just as you don't learn to drive by reading the *Highway Code* and being a passenger, although they're helpful starting points. You learn by observing, experiencing, trying, failing, trying again, getting better and eventually mastering it.

Given the essential nature of learning by replicating, and the role senior leaders play in creating culture, I've made this the largest chapter in the book. In my experience, this important element is the one most likely to be missing in organisations struggling with engagement. If you can't lead yourself and set the right example, you're never going to bring people along on the journey with you. You'll be expending a lot of effort trying to push resistant people forwards, rather than the effortless joy of leading willing people.

If you focus on this chapter, digest it, work through the exercises and thinking points and take full ownership of the ideas presented in it, you will be more than half way to creating a highly engaged workforce

When I led a team of leaders in Cape Town in a three day seminar centred around this one chapter, they joined me with passion and energy in implementing the ideas presented. As a result, their employee engagement scores linked to leadership rose from 59% to 74% in just six weeks.

The ideas in this book are not rocket science. Their gravity won't challenge you. It's their implementation and consistent use that need your attention.

The vital points to remember are:

- It must start with you

- Master these ideas first

- Be consistent; don't try them out for a few days then go back to a comfortable groove

- Share your vision with the team to get their inputs.

Once you've mastered these ideas, share them with your team. People thrive on this kind of knowledge, and when they see benefits not only in their work life, but their personal lives too, you will see big performance improvements in relatively short periods of time.

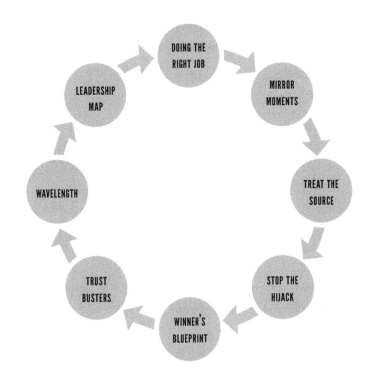

# Critical success factors

Leaders need to master eight critical skills in order to lead themselves first. We'll look at each stage in this chapter.

# Doing the right job

One of our shared human drivers is the need to feel self-directed. People want a sense of autonomy, to be master of their own ship. It's not entirely possible in a usual work context; there has to be direction setting by the organisation or you'd have chaos. But the degree to which self-direction could be handed over and isn't is the degree to which creativity, potential and results are limited.

So an obvious question to ask might be how should you lead to allow self-direction, and in doing so drive engagement and loyalty?

I use the analogy of an air traffic controller.

- They are vastly experienced and know a lot about aviation

- They issue instructions on altitude, direction, speed, etc.

- They are aware of individual planes in the context of overall air space

- They adjust quickly in response to ever changing conditions

- Their objective is to land the planes safely, in a certain order, on time

- They take control during a crisis and switch to become authoritarian to prevent disaster.

---

*Human beings have an innate inner drive to be autonomous, self-determined, and connected to one another. And when that drive is liberated, people achieve more and live richer lives.*

**DAN PINK**

---

But, crucially, an air traffic controller does not fly the planes.

Do your job, and let your teams do theirs. You are not the pilot; your role is to make them exceptional pilots. Get the best out of them - inspire them to want to join you on the journey and elevate their performance to such an extent that they can be the best. Land difficult messages in a way that leads to ownership of the problem and its solution without crushing the team's spirit. Paint a picture of a better way of being and working, inspire self-belief that it's possible and remove obstacles so the team can be about the business of making it a reality.

---

Micromanage: control every part, however small, of (an enterprise or activity).
**OXFORD DICTIONARY OF ENGLISH**

---

I have heard disengaged employees cite micromanagement as a reason for dissatisfaction on so many occasions. They sense a lack of trust, and that the leader thinks s/he knows better. It is crushing and dehumanising for employees. It appears that their leader is predicting a poor outcome before the task is even finished, which promotes an attitude of 'why should I bother?' The employees can eventually become wilfully resistant and obstructive.

In a survey by **Trinity Solutions Inc.**, **79%** of respondents had experienced micromanagement, either currently or in the past. Of those, **69%** said they'd considered changing jobs because of micromanagement and **36%** had actually changed jobs. Additionally, **73%** said being micromanaged interfered with their job performance, while **77%** said their morale was negatively impacted.

The more the leader tightens the reins, the worse the problem gets, leading to the exact opposite of what s/he wants. Performance and morale go down; poor attitudes and performance issues go up. People intentionally block as they look to take back a sense of control in whatever way they can. It's a predictable, albeit unsavoury, human behaviour.

The drive for self-direction is a powerful one. The great news is when you positively tap into it, you will begin to see big results in short periods of time.

# KEY ENGAGEMENT AUDIT – DOING THE RIGHT JOB

There will be an audit at the end of each section. Before moving on to the next section, take a moment to reflect on the key points and questions in the section you've just covered.

---

*You are what you do, not what you say you'll do.*

**CARL JUNG**

---

In what ways are you micromanaging? When aren't you micromanaging? In what ways are you under-delegating? How are you effectively delegating? If you're unsure, ask for feedback.

Who in your team are you micromanaging the most? Why? What will you do about it?

Who in your team are you micromanaging the least? What can you learn from that?

What's one way you could change this behaviour in yourself? In others? In what ways are you already a role model?

If you're not micromanaging, but others are, how could you positively influence that? What else can that teach you?

How could this be an area of dissatisfaction that causes people to leave your organisation?

What can you learn from that?

# Mirror moments

When it comes to employee engagement and loyalty, I have some good news and some bad news for you. In fact, it's the same news; it just depends how you look at it.

You are part of the problem. That may be difficult to hear, but it's true nonetheless.

It's not the staff, although they can test you with their ridiculous behaviour. It's not the organisation, although sometimes its policies hinder you. It's not another department, although they seem to block you at every turn for fun. It's not the mid-level managers, although they find it hard to implement your vision.

---

*What you do speaks so loudly that*
*I cannot hear what you're saying.*

**RALPH WALDO EMERSON**

---

Senior leaders in an organisation create the culture by virtue of the things they consistently do or say, or maybe don't do or say. It sets the tone, like water running over rock eventually shapes a groove. So if you're looking for the answers to the ever present questions 'Why are my people leaving?' or, more aptly, 'Why are my people disengaged?', the place to start is by holding up the mirror.

Thankfully, you are also part of the solution.

Nothing great was ever accomplished without there first being a significant level of discomfort with the current situation, so if the message above makes you uncomfortable, that's good. It means you're ready to progress.

In my experience, truly great leaders first and foremost ask what they could do differently. How could they interact with others more effectively? How have they contributed to communication issues, and in what ways could they improve next time? They consistently role model expected behaviours and own the odd moments when they don't. They see every interaction with their teams and others as an opportunity to help those people grow and flourish, even if they have to deliver a difficult message. And they share their time, experience and knowledge freely and without strings.

'Do as I say, not as I do' is the mantra of many failed leaders and poor organisational cultures.

I'm sure we've all observed leaders, with good intentions, act counter to the things they themselves would wish to observe in others. Those that have looked to drive the coaching culture in their organisations, for example, only to regularly cancel their own caching sessions at the last minute due to business pressures. Or those that genuinely wanted to drive engagement, but were too busy to spot good performance and give praise. Or how many meetings have been hijacked by ordinarily calm but now irate senior leaders demanding explanations for an off-track project.

It is wholly acceptable - necessary, in fact - to flag poor performance. You wouldn't be leading properly if you overlooked it, and your team knows that, but you have to regulate how your feedback is delivered. If you want to offload both barrels because you've reached the end of your tether, here are the circumstances when that is acceptable: never. If you want to course correct, develop and reset performance boundaries then you can truly call yourself a leader. How a leader does anything is much more powerful than that what or the why in the eyes of the people they lead.

If you're the kind of leader who cares enough about this issue to be reading this book, chances are high that most of the time you're level-headed. You only lose it every now and then. But 'every now and then' is magnified when you're a role model.

---

*Good intentions don't work.*

**JEFF BEZOS**

---

After an irate meeting as described earlier, I would follow up with the senior leader to provide some feedback. (I never knowingly walk past good or poor performance without calling it out. That's how I show respect to others.) S/he may initially be quite astonished that s/he has came across that way, but that's how we grow. And if we link it back to the poor engagement scores, and the fact that engagement filters down, I'm sure s/he would see how s/he would influence a positive change by being more emotionally controlled.

You've got to lead yourself first. Regulate your emotional responses, always have positive intentions, even behind the most challenging communications, and be the role model of engagement you want to see in your organisation.

As a leader, there are some days when you feel on top of the world. You know you've had a massive impact on someone and inspired them to be and do more than they thought possible. It's an amazing feeling; nothing beats it.

There are also days when the only thing stopping you from jumping out of the window is the fact it's sealed shut. Why? Because people are people, with all of their wonderful, surprising and sometimes frustrating characteristics, responses and mood swings.

What motivates and empowers one person doesn't work for the next person, and what motivates and empowers a person one day doesn't the next day. As workflow, business demands, customer interactions, team dynamics and hidden personal lives push and pull against one another, they create changing responses within people. But while it does make sense that our leadership approach is agile, I have found, after two decades of research, study, real world application, learning from mistakes, building on successes and role modelling excellence, that there are some fundamentals. If these are applied successfully, they form the solid foundation upon which legendary organisations can flourish, rock star teams can thrive, and individual loyalty is so fierce that work becomes a vibrant, highly engaging and energising place to be.

## KEY ENGAGEMENT AUDIT – MIRROR MOMENTS

How willing are you to accept that you are part of the engagement problem in your organisation? In what ways are you a champion of engagement? In the last two weeks, what situation could you have handled differently? What situation are you most proud of? What can you learn from that? What can you teach others about that?

Which behaviour of yours are you overlooking? What assumptions have you made about that? Which behaviours could others role model from you?

How could this be an area of dissatisfaction that causes people to leave your organisation? What can you learn from that?

# Treat the source

If you're consistently experiencing behavioural issues with your team or organisation, you need to have the courage and humility to hold the mirror up to yourself first to find the source.

After years of treating the downstream impacts of poor engagement: poor communication, low productivity, lack of ownership, poor morale, no coaching, etc., I've come to realise that there is a source that these impacts run from. If you treat the source, you solve most of the other issues that plague teams and organisations without effort.

You suddenly find that people knew all along how to communicate with each other, so you don't need to run the Communication Skills workshop. They either avoid relationship conflict (as opposed to task conflict where ideas are vigorously debated, which is healthy in an organisation) or they handle it with grace and ease, so you don't need to run the Managing Conflict workshop. They want to go over and above what's expected and apply discretionary effort, so you no longer need to grovel when you ask them to stay an extra five minutes - heaven forbid! All of a sudden, they arrive on time, have good attitudes and work in cohesive functioning teams with virtually no outer direction - cut the Courageous Conversations programme, too.

Ah, the Holy Grail. Does such a place exist? Emphatically, yes. I've seen it and replicated it many times, and so can you if you can get past the first hurdle: the knowing/doing gap.

---

*It's not what you know, it's what you do that counts.*

**LOU LUDWIG**

---

The great Bob Proctor coined the term 'knowing/doing gap'. It succinctly describes a problem faced by many people, not just leaders.

Let's use an analogy that I think most of us can relate to: getting fitter.

You want to lose a few extra pounds, maybe for a nice holiday or important meeting. You're super clear on the goal; you're motivated to take action; you're repeating to yourself, 'Looking good feels better than cake tastes'; you've dusted off your running shoes. You own this!

Well, you do for a few days, but by the weekend, apparently you've 'earned' a Chinese takeaway. Then real life closes in around you. You're staying late at work to finish your strategy document and things soon fall back into a comfortable groove.

So what's going on here? Why do our words and actions mismatch? To stick with our analogy, there are pros and cons to the effort of getting fitter, and there are pros and cons to staying the same. They're stacked on a set of scales: pros to getting fitter and cons to staying the same on one side, and cons to getting fitter and pros of staying the same on the other.

It might look like this:

| PROS TO GETTING FITTER | CONS TO GETTING FITTER |
|---|---|
| Feel better, clothes will fit, sense of personal pride, enjoy time with kids more, attract a partner, etc. | Too tired after work to go to the gym, may feel like an obligation, hassle of getting to the gym, buying expensive workout gear, etc. |
| **CONS TO STAYING THE SAME** | **PROS TO STAYING THE SAME** |
| Feel bad about myself, ill health, out of breath, others may not respect me as much, lack discipline, etc. | Can relax and enjoy the time off I deserve, have a lie in, enjoy nice meals out with my friends, save money on expensive gym, etc. |

Whichever side of the scales is heavier or more compelling, that's the side that prevails. And it only has to be fractionally heavier. If the left hand side is heavier, you will focus on and achieve fitness. If the right side is more compelling, you will lose interest and revert back to your old ways.

---

*If I had four hours to chop down a tree, I'd spend
the first two hours sharpening the axe.*

**ABRAHAM LINCOLN**

---

Before I introduce new thinking points about tipping the scales in your favour, let's consider how you can already do that with virtually no effort. We often overlook the low hanging fruit.

What do you know you should do, but aren't doing, that would help drive engagement? For example, you might know regular coaching sessions, including skip levels, would help, but you don't plan them in advance, and you willingly cancel them at the last minute if something else comes up. However, you expect coaching to be part of the culture in your teams. Perhaps you dominate in team meetings, speaking first, and loudest, and you don't involve the team in shaping how goals will be achieved. Ideally the leader sets the what and why, and the team shapes the how to achieve the goal, e.g. asking how can we fix this issue? Who has experienced this before? Who could we speak to? etc.

Do you take opportunities to praise individual or team effort, or are you so busy you assume they know you're pleased with their performance? Is your door often closed, or are you visible and accessible? Is it apparent when people are interrupting you?

Things like this are just as easy to get right as get wrong. In isolation they don't make much difference, but when added together over time, they do. So before trying anything new, start with the basics. Do them well and do them consistently.

## KEY ENGAGEMENT AUDIT – TREAT THE SOURCE

Now you've surfaced the quick wins, what needs to happen to implement them? Who could support you in that? What are you consistently getting right? How will this benefit you, your team and the organisation positively?

How could this be an area of dissatisfaction that causes people to leave your organisation? What can you learn from that?

# Stop the hijack

When I mention emotional intelligence in my seminars and meetings, I'm often met with looks of disdain. The mere mention of the word 'emotion' in a work setting is enough to send many leaders into a mild panic. They see it as the warm and fuzzy stuff that HR is always going on about, but in the real world of work, emotions play no part. They are too subjective, 'out there' and new age.

---

*When you react, you are giving away your power,*
*the situation controls you. When you respond, you*
*are staying in control of the situation yourself.*

**BOB PROCTOR TRAINING DVD**

---

That is until I explain the science that sits behind emotional intelligence (EQ).

Special thanks to my colleague, **Brian Pabst**, for sharing his wisdom with me on the subject, and for the many stimulating and illuminating conversations we've had on EQ.

So what is emotional intelligence (EQ)?

---

*The capability of individuals to recognize their own, and other people's emotions, to discriminate between different feelings and label them appropriately, to use emotional information to guide thinking and behavior, and to manage and/or adjust emotions to adapting environments or achieve one's goal(s).*

**WIKIPEDIA**

---

Of course technical skills matter, but they mostly represent an entry bar for positions. A person either has them or not, and can develop them to a certain level required for the job.

IQ is not so much what you know, but your ability to learn. It's fixed throughout life (unlike the volume of information we gain over our lives, which of course does change). EQ, on the other hand, is a skill like any other skill. It can be learned and mastered. The Holy Grail is to possess both

EQ matters more when it comes to leadership. Without EQ, a person can have the best training in the world, an incisive, analytical mind, and an endless supply of smart ideas, but s/he still won't make a great leader.

Take a moment to recall a truly inspirational role model leader you've known. What was it about them that you admired? In my experience, it tends to be how a person is, rather than what they know, that makes them stand out, e.g. their ability to see things from another's perspective, deliver challenging messages in inspiring ways, or their calmness in the face of obvious pressure. All these are emotional skills, not intelligence.

---

*...the feelings, beliefs, perceptions and values that people hold when they engage with any business. It's the emotional assets in your organisation that determine whether or not people will work well for you, buy from you, employ you and enter into business with you.*

**ROCHEMARTIN.CO.UK**

---

As a leader, you will inspire or demoralise others by how effectively you manage your own emotional energy and responses to situations. Having high EQ is the epitome of Focus On Yourself First.

It is very apparent to me when a leader has high EQ. I can see it in the energy and enthusiasm of their team to innovate, solve problems and perform in a self-directed way. Teams are a reflection of the leader.

Every relationship that you have in your organisation, and outside, is an asset and an investment. People in your organisation are intellectual and emotional investors. Every day they bring their minds, potential, motivation and hearts to work. And if they don't, your business is at risk. Don't over-engineer solutions to the engagement problem. It couldn't be easier: be the example you want to see, consistently and willingly.

If you believe that emotions play no role in a work context, and that you can somehow outthink them from 9am to 5pm every day, then you are disregarding thousands of years of human evolution, in particular a part of the brain called the limbic system which contains the small but powerful amygdala.

I'm not going to get too 'sciencey' here, just enough to demonstrate emotional intelligence in the realm of logic and reason. Here are a few brief descriptors to assist. More detailed information is easily available via the internet.

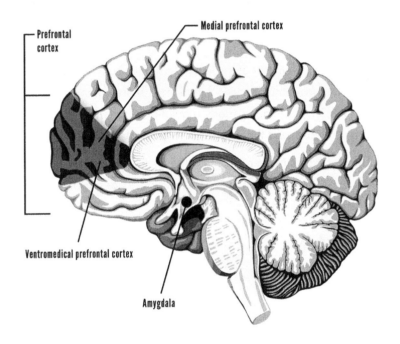

# Prefrontal cortex

This region of the brain is involved in planning complex cognitive behaviour, personality expression, decision making, and moderating social behaviour and impulses. It is in charge of abstract thinking and thought analysis. It is also responsible for regulating behaviour. This includes mediating conflicting thoughts, making choices between right and wrong, and predicting the probable outcomes of actions or events. In evolutionary terms, it's the newer, higher thinking region of the brain.

## The limbic system

This is a complex system of nerves and networks in the brain, involving several areas near the edge of the cortex concerned with instinct and mood. It links the higher and lower thinking regions of the brain and deals with three key functions: emotions, memories and arousal/stimulation.

The primary elements of the limbic system include the hippocampus (involved in memory function), thalamus (sensory perception and movement), hypothalamus (body regulation, e.g. temperature and hormone release) and the amygdala (emotions).

The limbic system overall controls the basic emotions such as fear, pleasure, anger, and drives such as hunger, sexual desire, dominance and care of offspring.

## The amygdala

This is the king of the limbic system when it comes to our emotional responses to things, people and situations. It's like an electrical switching station, dealing with fear and threat detection. Inputs from other parts of the system converge in the amygdala, and it controls the output: our response.

The amygdala takes the sensory information being received, such as sight and sound - 'What's the external situation/stimulus I'm experiencing?'; memory - 'Has this happened before? What was the outcome then? How did I handle it?'; and previous associations

- 'This person shouted at me before, I assume they will again'. It then determines if there is a threat.

In a situation which threatens our safety, the Flight or Fight response kicks in and takes over the logic centre in the prefrontal cortex. We usually don't have a true threat to our physical safety, but distress and fear can cause this same response to kick in. When it does, we experience emotional extremes and are unaware that our logic is ineffective or limited.

This is a vital message to take on board if we are to be effective leaders, because this part of our brain - operating with good intentions to save us from fear, risk or distress - temporarily overrides the logical part of our brain in doing so. It literally hijacks us.

## The amygdala hijack

Amygdala hijack is an immediate and overwhelming emotional response out of proportion to the stimulus.

Think about a recent event where you lost control for a moment. Maybe in a traffic jam, or argument with a spouse, or you lost your temper with your children. Afterwards, when the dust had settled, was there a part of you that knew you'd overreacted? That the other person had pushed your buttons to the point of an emotional explosion, and maybe you said and did things that in hindsight were a bit much?

Why couldn't you have decided that in the moment and avoided the distress? Because the amygdala, sensing some sort of emotional threat, took over. It hijacked you, and for a while you were not yourself - literally. Logic gave way to overwhelming emotions.

Now think of that in a work context. Chances are you're mostly emotionally unaffected by the actions and behaviours around you. But what of *those* meetings that drive you mad? And *that* person you avoid because of how they make you feel? Or *the* team member who always pushes your buttons? Our buttons are different, but we all have them.

For those particular people or situations, you need an effective way to improve your EQ. It's impossible to disconnect this powerful, ancient part of your brain completely, but possible to increase awareness, decrease reactivity, and reduce the situations that affect you.

Perhaps you're uncomfortably aware that you often respond negatively or emotionally. If you are, you're demonstrating a high EQ by acknowledging it. The good news is now you know, you can easily do something about it. In terms of driving engagement within your team, this one element could be the key you've been looking for.

Something I hear a lot from leaders when we discuss this subject is: 'I can control my response. If I'm feeling frustrated or angry on the inside, it never shows.' Perhaps you're thinking the same.

You may be able to contain it a bit in terms of the external evidence that you're angry or frustrated, but it's still happening in your brain, overriding logic and clear thinking and making you react rather than respond. Plus we're all experts in body language. You may think you've disguised it, but people know - your team especially as they have a vast bank of experience of how you have reacted before to compare and contrast.

The key isn't to try to hide it; it's to change how you're responding in the first place so you don't have to. To lead yourself first, you need to be **aware** of the issue, **care** enough to want to change it and **dare** to incorporate new patterns of thinking and behaviour so you can be a truly excellent role model leader.

# Improving your EQ

How do we learn anything? From learning to walk and speak right through to wherever you are now, you have learned by the same process. The first time you try any new skill is the hardest.

Let's take learning to drive as an example as most people can relate to it. The first time you drove was very challenging, involving a new set of manoeuvres and movements. It felt completely alien. Now, if you've been driving for a while, I bet you don't even think about it. It's an automatic skill.

---

*Neurons that fire together wire together.*

**DONALD HEBB**

---

The learning of skills to the point of automatic habit starts from the first time you attempt something. Neurons in your brain fire together in a particular way and order to represent the new skill or thought. If you try the skill or thought again, the same neurons fire together again and become a bit stronger. A third attempt, a bit stronger, and so on until eventually a new neural network is formed, or hardwired. EQ, like anything else, can be learned.

Improving emotional intelligence means a lot of different things, but scientifically and physiologically, it means the communication pathways between the amygdala (emotions) and prefrontal cortex (logic) are broad and healthy. In other words, the neural pathways between the two parts of the brain are strengthened.

It's scientifically possible to measure emotional intelligence and, as with all skills, to improve it over time by strengthening the pathways in our minds.

# Take a test

You wouldn't train once for a marathon and believe that was enough. It takes time and persistent effort. It's the same with developing EQ. Take a thirty-day test and see for yourself the benefits to be gained.

Spend fifteen minutes per day acting and reflecting on the following:

**Knowledge.** There is an ocean of information about EQ on great videos on the internet or in books. Find something to read or view on the subject daily. Take the bits that resonate, discard the rest. Implement one new positive idea, however small, during that day and reflect on it in the evening.

**Self-awareness.** Spend some time each day observing yourself. Imagine you're a third party viewing yourself in a meeting or team interaction. How do you react? What's going through your mind when certain people are speaking? Are you containing rising frustration? If you're experiencing an emotional response, stop to ask yourself:

- What is the specific emotion I'm feeling? E.g. annoyed, frustrated, worried?

- How do I feel? Let down? Disrespected?

- About what specifically do I feel it?

- Why do I feel like that?

Rational thinking relies on and therefore reactivates the prefrontal cortex. This then reduces the emotional response enough to regain control.

For example, if you're feeling annoyed because a certain colleague (let's call him Mike) didn't get a report to you on time, and it's not the first time it's happened despite Mike always demanding that you get reports to him on time, now you can have a calm, rational conversation with him. Clearly he does need to improve his performance, and he is more likely to do so when it's discussed in a rational way.

**Perceptual experimentation.** Ahead of a meeting or discussion where you predict a negative outcome, play the event through in your mind a few times with an imagined positive and productive outcome. After the event, reflect on the outcome.

**Course correction.** Probably the most challenging task, but also the most powerful in forming new habits. Where possible, catch yourself in the moment of rising emotions (before it's got to the point of emotional hijack) and ask yourself a provocative question such as, 'Am I allowing the limbic system to take over my rational thought?' or 'Am I being unreasonable in any part of my thinking?' or 'How might this look from the other person's vantage point?' Like the example above, because you have to think and reason to ask the question and find an answer, you force activity in the prefrontal cortex.

You have nothing to lose and everything to gain from this experiment, so give it your best shot. Each time you think or act upon developing your EQ, the neural pathways between the emotional and logical parts of the brain strengthen.

---

*Change your thoughts and you'll change your world*

**NORMAN PEALE**

---

I work with some of the greatest companies and leaders in the world. I get to travel overseas to amazing places and meet exceptionally talented and inspirational people, all while being true to my life's purpose: 'Helping people be and do more than they could ever imagine'. It is pretty cool, to be honest.

But everyone's job has its frustrations. My own frustrations include 4am starts to get to airports, weekends away from home, anxiety about flying, time zone adjustments, poor sleep, lost luggage, and so on.

I could choose to have those frustrations front of mind, so blown up in my thinking that I begin to believe that it is the sum total of my experience: a job that causes me inconvenience and steals my time and energy. Eventually, I give myself a title: victim. Boo hoo, poor me.

Or I could choose to be enthused and inspired by the reason I'm going through the frustrations in the first place. The frustrations remain, but they're not my main focus. I direct my thoughts elsewhere, and in so doing have a less frustrating overall experience.

**Option A** - focus on frustrations = frustrating experience

**Option B** - focus on an inspiring vision = inspirational experience

It's not the event itself, it's the meaning that you choose to give it that ultimately affects the quality of your life and your leadership.

## KEY ENGAGEMENT AUDIT – STOP THE HIJACK

Which situations/people frustrate you? If they no longer frustrated you, what impact would that have on you/them/the team?

In what ways are you an EQ role model to others? How would others describe your EQ? If this is difficult to answer, ask for feedback.

How would you describe the overall EQ culture in your organisation? What impact is that having on performance and engagement? What, if anything, needs to be done about it?

Which element(s) of the thirty day EQ test resonate as the most important for you? How will you implement and track the test?

Which positive thoughts do you choose to have? Which negative thoughts are you allowing yourself to focus on?

How could this be an area of dissatisfaction that causes people to leave your organisation? What can you learn from that?

# Winner's blueprint

A mentor told me something many years ago and I've never forgotten it:

'As a leader, you don't get to choose whether you're a role model or not, just whether you're a good one or not.'

Wise words indeed, and especially important when considering employee engagement.

---

*Setting an example is not the main means of influencing another, it is the only means.*

**ALBERT EINSTEIN**

---

You are always role modelling. The things you do and say, or don't do and say, over time become the way others behave. Teams are always a reflection of the leader.

Some years ago, I was working with a senior leader to drive the coaching culture in the business. He was a standout leader, particularly when it came to the development of his people. I always enjoyed working with him. We were having a review meeting, and as we neared the end of our allocated time, we hadn't quite finished. Without a word, he picked up the phone, called the Operations Manager and informed him that he would have to postpone their coaching session so we could continue to discuss the coaching culture.

I'm sure I don't have to explain the irony of this counter-productive behaviour to you. Even the best of us, armed with the best of intentions, gets it wrong sometimes. And what we say and do, however unintentional, has an impact on those we lead.

When it comes to copying either our role-models' instructions or our experiences with them, experiences win. You can tell your people to do something until you're blue in the face, but if you are not doing that thing yourself, there won't be widespread adoption. And if you call out underperformance in an area you yourself fall short in, the injustice of it will pull your team apart.

It's often the little things that count, like cancelling a coaching session, as over time the cumulative effect of them can be devastating.

So ask yourself:

○ What kind of role model do you want to be?

○ In what ways are you already a positive role model?

○ In what ways are you role modelling the wrong things?

○ What's getting in your way?

○ What are you going to do about it?

○ What difference would it make to morale and engagement?

I understand the push and pull of a senior leader's life. We have the big strategic plans and discussions to orchestrate and manage.

We have one eye fixed firmly on the horizon, like the captain of a ship charting a safe course, navigating miles out to sea, not just a few hundred metres in front of them. The other eye is fixed on the here and now - the immediate and ever changing landscape. No point having charted a safe course only to run aground on rocks coming out of harbour.

It's demanding and challenging for sure. But in all the activity - the chaos, as sometimes it seems - you simply can't forget the team. Once they sense that they are not one of your priorities, they stop trying.

---

*Your team know how you feel towards them
and the value you place on them by the priority
you put on time with them.*

---

Team time, both individual and as a group, is as woven into the fabric of team performance and engagement as carbon is to steel. It doesn't even have to represent the majority of your time; it just needs to get your attention first of all, and not be the thing that's cut the moment another business pressure occurs. Only genuine emergencies can prevent team time.

*Set yourself and your leader-level reports some minimum operating standards when it comes to time with and attention on your people:*

**Connect with your team**. And as many of their reports as you can. This can be a simple few minutes of chit-chat to more formal 1:1s, but do it, and do it **daily.**

**Spend the first thirty minutes of your day with your team.** Forget email. Have a cursory glance at the inbox to ensure there are no genuine emergencies that need your immediate attention, then walk away. Usually I hear a sharp intake of breath when I share that, but

I guarantee that **everyone** who has gone on to try it has reported a positive effect. Orchestrate your day/diary to make this happen. Team time doesn't have to represent a large amount of time, but make it the first thing you do, the priority. What gets prioritised, gets done.

**Spend at least one hour a day in 1:1s/development/coaching.** I spend 50% of my time on this.

**Never walk past good or poor performance without calling it out.** How, where, when, etc. will depend on various things, but do it. The need for calling out good performance is covered in the next chapter. The reason and method for calling out poor performance is covered in the chapter 'Raise The Bar'.

# Control your life

I've been fortunate to take some stellar teams to the very edges of their capability, helping them to embrace new ways of thinking and approaching their work, inspiring them to see a bright vision for their teams and results. It's the most rewarding work I could imagine doing. But I'm often surprised how short lived the enthusiasm is and how quickly the results revert back again after the development.

There's certainly no lack of desire to improve, but there is something all people have in common that acts as an invisible barrier to improvement. Its powerful influence is outside of the conscious awareness of most people, but the limitations it places on them, their lives, their results, their happiness and fulfilment are monumental.

And to be able to lead yourself, you must understand it and its impact on you.

Deep in each of us lies a blueprint of who we are, how we operate and the limits we perceive ourselves to have. It's a self-image deep inside our conscious minds, not the image we portray to the outside world, that tells us what job we should have, the income we deserve, the results we should produce, how we manage our time, how we interact with the people around us, where we see ourselves in the future, and so on. It determines what's important to us in our day to day experience and what we're willing to do to achieve it. It's learned at an early age and it rarely changes significantly over a person's lifetime. Simply put, it controls our life.

---

*Self-image sets the boundaries of*
*individual accomplishment.*
**MAXWELL MALTZ**

---

If a person's blueprint, or internal self-image, is that of someone who is an average performer, it will keep them operating at around that level. Not below that level, which of course is a good thing, but critically not above it either.

When I first heard and considered that point, a lower and upper limit on achievement, it blew my mind. An invisible barrier to success had been controlling and directing my life – my choices and decisions; what I chose to focus my time and effort on; my levels of curiosity and creativity; my interactions with others; how motivated I was to stay the course.

If a person learns how to become a better or star performer, they may well improve for a short period of time, but if the approach and resulting positive outcomes deviate too far from their internal blueprint, the changes won't last. It's like a thermostat at home. The room can operate within a band of temperature. If it's too cold, the heating will come on, and once the desired level is reached, the boiler goes off. We operate the same way.

Maxwell Maltz wrote an incredible book on this, *Psycho-Cybernetics*, in1960. In it he explains why if a person elevates their performance above the higher limit they have internally set for themselves, remarkably, their unconscious mind will attempt to 'rectify' the perceived deviation, possibly sabotaging their performance or zooming in on a false reason to quit a new job, so that a comfortable rebalance can be found.

This is important for you personally, and also for your teams. We'll come back to it in the chapter 'Raise The Bar'.

---

*We think in secret and it comes to pass,*
*environment is but our looking-glass.*

**JAMES ALLEN**

---

The key, then, is to cultivate an internal image of being successful (e.g. better results, successful and engaged teams, *that* promotion, developing confidence, starting a business, etc.) before we begin to change external factors and behaviours. It's the internal self-image that determines our goals, our longer term habitual actions, our decisions, our motivation levels, our persistence in the face of adversity – in fact, all manner of things that separate successful, happy, self-determined people from the rest.

If you go to the root cause, the self-image we all hold of ourselves, and improve that, you will be astonished how far you could go, and how quickly. To quote from **Price Pritchett's** small but mighty book, $You^2$, you can easily make 'high velocity moves that result in explosive jumps in personal performance that put you far beyond the next logical step'. I love that, and recommend the book most highly.

# KEY ENGAGEMENT AUDIT – WINNER'S BLUEPRINT

What level of success are you comfortable operating in? If your boss's boss left the organisation, would you apply for the role? If not, setting aside any apparent skill/knowledge gap or other factor, e.g. it would mean a relocation, how is your internal voice holding you back?

Who in your team is being held back by their internal blueprint? How do you know? An example may be one of your top performers who doesn't go for promotions because they don't perceive they have the skill or readiness for the role. What steps could you take to surface and positively impact their view?

Can you clearly imagine and picture the kind of organisation and teams you're trying to create? (Link back to the exercise in the opening chapter.) What internal chatter is telling you it's not possible? How can you focus on this to embed a positive self-image?

What do you need to think and believe about yourself and your own capabilities to inspire others to elevate themselves to their full potential? What impact would that have on morale, performance and engagement?

How could this be an area of dissatisfaction that causes people to leave your organisation? What can you learn from that?

# Trust Busters

Without trust, you're going nowhere. Successful organisations and strong teams are built on in. Other organisations and teams drown without it.

**What is trust?** There is no definitive answer. I'm sure you have your own, but the components and building blocks are:

- Authenticity - being yourself, showing who you are, having a voice you stand behind

- Vulnerability - admitting mistakes, asking for help, being OK with not knowing all the answers, highlighting expertise beyond your own, asking for feedback

- Consistency - calling out good and poor performance, no favourites, transparent processes, behaving in the way you expect others to behave.

One of the things I loved about my time with Amazon was the customer obsession. It's not a statement on a staff noticeboard that doesn't get looked at; these guys mean in. It's quite breath-taking to see the lengths they'll go to in order to delight customers - if you're one, I'm sure you understand. They ruthlessly seek out ways to improve and are exceptional at learning from mistakes and fixing them so they stay fixed.

Amazon refers to issues that affect a customer's experience or perception of them as 'Trust Busters'.

I have often wondered what would happen if organisations had the same level of obsession for their employees. What if every decision was passed through a filter that asked, 'What impact will this have on staff? How will it affect morale? If an adverse effect is unavoidable, how will we mitigate it? How should we communicate it? Does it take us closer to or further away from a culture of engagement?'

# Building trust

For a leader, establishing and maintaining trust is critical when it comes to engagement and loyalty.

Trust is being established or broken in all of the smallest moments when we're leading. One of the most powerful activities I've ever come across to build trust is from Patrick Lencioni's wonderful book, *The Five Dysfunctions of a Team*. A phenomenal read, one of my favourites.

The activity, which I've used with many teams to achieve phenomenal results, is a feedback activity. Each person in the team provides every other person with one piece of positive, reinforcing feedback, and one piece of developmental feedback. It's done face to face, in a group setting, and you need a third party to facilitate it, someone not participating, so the full weight of the activity is shared among the team. The balanced nature of the feedback avoids the 'combat zone', while the shared experience of opening up and being courageous enough to give the feedback, and vulnerable enough to accept it, creates an irresistible, almost tribal bond.

And as the leader, you go first in receiving your feedback. This powerful demonstration of vulnerability and 'we're all in this together' smashes through any resistance and fear about the activity. I can always see and sense the energy shift in the room during and just after this first step. It's liberating.

I highly recommend the book, the team assessment and the activity. It sounds daunting, but it has never been less than outstanding.

# Trust and engagement

Trust is a vital element of engagement, and it also filters down, not up. When people trust you, it's not the same as them liking you, although the two do often go hand in hand. It means that they respect you.

Even if you're delivering a tough message or implementing an unpopular policy, where trust exists, adoption will follow.

When you are consistent in actions that build trust, you're role modelling them, setting a clear track for others to follow and the expectation that they will do so. If you expect on-time project delivery, you must deliver your projects on time. If you expect respectful communication, you must use it. If you expect your team to be willing to give feedback to and receive it from one another, you must be willing to do so too.

## KEY ENGAGEMENT AUDIT – TRUST BUSTERS

How do you already establish and maintain trust? What's the first step? What could you teach others about that?

What could you stop or start to build trust further? Who could teach you about that?

What's the biggest step? What do you need to own? What do you need to highlight? What's *that* conversation you know you need to have?

If you were more employee obsessed, what would that look, sound and feel like? How would that impact performance, morale and engagement?

Authentic, vulnerable, consistent – which one do you rock? Which one needs your attention?

What's the climate of trust in the organisation overall? How do you know? What impact is that having? What needs to happen?

How could this be an area of dissatisfaction that causes people to leave your organisation? What can you learn from that?

# Wavelength

To be an effective leader, you need to have engaging, meaningful and productive relationships with all types of people. It is an essential skill. So why is it that with some people you click and with others you clunk?

If, like me, you can remember the pre-digital days of manually tuning in a radio, you know that to appreciate the channel fully, you needed to get it spot on. Even 5% crackle was enough to be frustrating. Even though you could hear the song or DJ, you weren't wholly engaged as the 5% distracted you.

The ability to tune in to other people's communication preferences and adapt your approach can make the difference in engaging and inspiring them. Once you're tuned in to each other's wavelength, there is an easy rapport, a common understanding. As leader, your ability to influence and engage others positively is greatly enhanced.

---

*The key to successful leadership today is*
*influence, not authority.*

**KEN BLANCHARD**

---

As a leader, you could tell your reports what to do. Maybe you do just that. If so, how is that working out in the longer term? Does it engage your team? Lead to greater ownership? Develop skill, autonomy and mastery in the role?

In the distant past, that's exactly what I did, but I was constantly swimming against the tide and getting nowhere fast. Very frustrating.

In my work, I meet people from different levels of an organisation, and I need to be able to influence them from the get go. Leaders at this level don't believe me because I say so.

Exceptional leaders exert **resonant influence**: a combination of authority and expertise, relationship building, and the desire and skill to get on someone's wavelength quickly.

Let's think about the different types of influence.

# Authority influence

'I'm the boss, I've got the title, you do as I say!'

In practice, it's usually a lot more subtle than this (although not always). The leader wants a last minute report, a project update, to change the shift patterns, new business targets, etc. The report may provide their own insights, inputs or objections, but in the main, what the leader wants gets done, mainly because s/he is the leader. But not necessarily because s/he has the better ideas or bigger priorities.

We tend to look up to positions and titles with a sense of reverence, obedience and sometimes even fear, and the authority influencer nurtures this tendency. It works well in times of crisis; with inexperienced teams who need a lot of direction; where the culture is hierarchical; when a leader is leading people through a big change; as a short-term approach. But it can represent a problem when the leader is plain wrong and can't see or won't admit it; when experienced teams aren't involved in shaping decisions, setting direction and formulating solutions; when authority and the 'just do it' message is used to micro manage and belittle people; if it's the long term influencing style.

# Relationship influence

'We've known/worked with each other for a while and I like and trust you.'

It may have taken some time, but you've got to a stage where there is mutual trust and respect. You've 'scratched each-other's backs', and the likability factor has grown as a result. At this stage, neither party wants to damage the relationship. As a leader, you seek out, listen and respond to inputs from such a report and look to come to mutually beneficial outcomes.

This type of influence works well with more experienced teams; where it's OK for the outcome to take a little longer; where both parties bring experience, knowledge and creativity to the situation; when the leader is far removed from the sharp end of the organisation (and therefore can't 'tell' as much). It also works well with peer/upward influencing. It can represent a problem when the relationship hasn't had time to form properly; when protecting the relationship is put above the right outcome; when a quick and decisive decision is needed (not death by committee); where both parties have divergent views, which can lead to stalemate or the wrong party conceding too much.

# Resonant influence

So, what if you don't have authority to wield? Or you do, but you want to create loyal followers rather than resentful workers? Or the relationship is important to you, but not more important than achieving successful outcomes? What if you've just met a person/team and you haven't had the time to let the relationship form? What if they have a completely different way of working and style to you?

Developing **resonant influence** is the answer. It's the key to getting on people's wavelength no matter who they are in relation to you (with or without authority), how long you've known each other and how your styles match or mismatch.

It incorporates four simple but effective elements:

1. **Consider the situation and desired outcomes from the other party's viewpoint.** This allows you to look for win/win outcomes authentically.

2. **Understand your own preferred communication style.** It's important to distinguish here between preference and ability. We can all have ability in each communication style, but it's our and others' innate preferences that can help us to get on each other's wavelength.

3. **Quickly and accurately identify the other person's preferred style**. For example, are they a facts or ideas person? Is their language rational (I think) or emotional (I feel)? Do they rely on gut instinct or proof? Is their focus task or people?

4. **Make small but important adaptations to your approach.** Speak their language, enter their world and resonate with one another.

Think about the different types of computers we have: PCs, laptops, Macs, phones, tablets. On the surface they share a lot of similarities: they process and store data, give us access to information, allow us to send communication, etc. But the way they do it is quite different.

It's the same with people. On the surface we all seem to act in broadly similar ways, but in our internal worlds are surprisingly different.

Look at the list below and ask yourself how you usually prefer to think/act. This doesn't mean you can't flex the other way; it's just your natural tendency.

- Loud vs quiet
- Task vs people
- Information vs ideas
- My opinion vs your opinion
- Rational vs emotional
- Do it vs think about it
- Instinct vs proof
- Vision vs reality
- Formal vs informal
- Immediate vs reflective.

Other people can share a lot, sometimes all, of your preferences. These are the people you find you click with easily. Communication is natural.

Where there is a lot of difference, that crackle can impact your ability to tune in to one another. Making small changes can have a big impact.

For example, imagine that you're someone who is a creative, intuitive big picture thinker. You get things done fast. Facts and evidence aren't very important to you as your instincts are good and you're right a lot of the time. You're communicating with someone who is precise, logical, likes to see things from all angles to have the facts and data to hand and take time before making a considered judgment. How would you speak to them?

Remember, as the leader, you have to be the one who adapts.

**Communication option A:** 'We need to get creative, think outside the box. Let's not be held back by how it's been done before; let's get cracking and make history!'

**Communication option B:** 'I've got a clear idea of where I want us to go, and I'd like to rely on your attention to detail and organisational skills to help us get there in a logical way.'

I'm sure if the creative type in our example heard option A, they'd tune right in. But option A wouldn't get the logical person on board. They would of course intellectually understand it, but it wouldn't be as compelling as option B.

The difference in language is the difference between 95% tuned in and 100% tuned in. It's not difficult to do and can be thought about in advance of conversations.

There are numerous models in the market today that lend themselves to this subject, e.g. DiSC, Insights Discovery and Social Styles. They are all highly effective, and I recommend you research them, but for our purpose you don't need such an in depth understanding.

Communication preference is a chunky subject. I do a deeper dive in the chapter 'Raise The Bar' in the context of courageous conversations, but here are three high impact communication adaptations to get you quickly and powerfully on to another person's wavelength:

**Use their preferred timeframe at the start of the conversation**. For example, link back to past experiences with Analysers before speaking about the vision. The reverse is true for the Inspirers, who need an end-game anchor in the future to think about before present plans are discussed.

**Consider how each style in the table above likes things at work**. Get right to the point with Commanders and be crisp and direct. Take longer with Harmonisers in a more open and relaxed setting. Take your time with the rapport, which must be genuine.

**Use their language**. Say the Strengths words shown in the table above, or words like them, in the opening part of your conversation.

To summarise:

| COMMANDER | INSPIRER | HARMONISER | ANALYSER |
|---|---|---|---|
| **FIVE WORDS TO DESCRIBE ME** | | | |
| Strong-willed<br>Determined<br>Competitive<br>Decisive<br>Assertive | Sociable<br>Enthusiastic<br>Optimistic<br>Creative<br>Intuitive | Caring<br>Patient<br>Co-operative<br>Friendly<br>Supportive | Precise<br>Logical<br>Formal<br>Structured<br>Organised |
| **HOW I LIKE IT IN WORK** | | | |
| Fast pace, high risk, results focused, busy and formal, direct and to the point | Options open, working towards a bigger picture, fun and stimulating | Low risk, time to reflect, friendly and supportive, relationships valued | Cautious, see all angles, systematic, finish projects, work alone, expertise valued |
| **PREFERRED TIMEFRAME TO OPERATE IN** | | | |
| Present | Future | Close past, near future | Past |
| **STRENGTHS** | | | |
| Gets the job done, delivers results, makes decisions others can't or won't, solves issues | Ideation, energy and motivation, positive can-do attitude, handles big workloads | Holds teams together, build trust and respect, boosts morale, good listener and supporter | Accurate, high-quality work, meets deadlines, data analysis, highly focused and reliable |
| **PITFALLS** | | | |
| Dominates, intolerant of others, puts results over relationships | Lacks attention to detail, easily bored, can be overly emotional | Slow to make decisions, avoids difficult conversations | Appears detached, puts own work ahead of team's, can be negative |

We like and resonate with people who are like us, and we judge that based on how the person mostly acts, what they tend to speak about, how they speak about it and the specific words they use.

The adaptations can be small, but they go a long way when it comes to sharing understanding and driving engagement. I recommend you arrange a training session on the subject of communication preference for you and your team. It's highly illuminating in itself, and yields real team performance and cohesive results.

---

# KEY ENGAGEMENT AUDIT – WAVELENGTH

Do you lean more towards authority influence (tell) or relationship influence (collaborate)? In what ways/circumstances do your communication preferences serve you and build trust and engagement? In what ways/circumstances do they hinder you and break trust and engagement?

What are you prepared to do/give up to improve? What do you expect others to do/give up to improve? How can you influence that?

How do your communication preferences supported you as leader? Who is your role model in this? What can you learn from them?

Who are you not 'tuned in' to? What can you observe about their communication preferences? What small adaptations could you make?

How could this be an area of dissatisfaction that causes people to leave your organisation? What can you learn from that?

# The leadership map

When was the last time you actively sought to prove yourself wrong and challenge your thinking? In my experience, it's so unlikely to have happened that even the question seems odd. That's certainly how I felt the first time I was asked it. Why would I want to prove myself wrong?

When do any of us acknowledge that our firmly held beliefs and opinions might not be right? It's much more likely that we hold them to be so true that they feel to us like indisputable facts. They are not.

This information tends to be the most hidden aspect of ourselves as leaders - in fact, as human beings. An uncomfortable mirror-moment for sure. To explain it in a sentence: we see what we expect to see, not what is there in reality. This has profound impact on the quality of our leadership.

For example, if we accept that an element of building trust is being able to admit when we're wrong, how can we do that if we're not looking for what's wrong? And if we want to develop EQ, we must be willing to see things from other people's perspectives and accept that their views are worthy of consideration.

In most quality newspapers, we find a mixture of negative and positive stories. I don't know anyone who reads an entire newspaper, so how do we decide what to read? An interesting photo or headline will no doubt capture our attention. But what other forces are at work that draws our gaze and holds our interest? Stated simply, if our outlook in life is generally towards the negative, we will be more drawn to the negative stories in the newspaper, because they reinforce our view of the world. The opposite is true if our outlook on life is generally optimistic.

From a cognitive science perspective, this is referred to a confirmation bias. It is defined as 'the tendency to interpret new evidence as confirmation of one's existing beliefs or theories'. As humans, we're constantly striving to prove we're right about everything and everyone. We look for information that backs us up, not that which makes us question ourselves. Feeling wrong feels bad. We then fall into the self-justification trap where we tell ourselves convenient stories, backed up by 'evidence', about the way we're behaving towards people and situations, further reinforcing the cycle.

---

*It ain't what you don't know that gets you into trouble.*
*It's what you know for sure that just ain't so.*

**MARK TWAIN**

---

This can have a big influence on how we lead. It hides the uncomfortable truth about ourselves and distorts our view of others.

Our need to be right is as prevalent as it is damaging. It is deeply embedded in our culture, organisations and families. It can become a collective belief system and we never even pause to consider it.

As leaders, we need to be aware of and question this and the impact it has on us, our teams and our organisations.

---

*It's so, because I think it is so.*

**LYNNE NAMKA**

---

This one aspect of human behaviour has led to more conflict, disharmony, war and atrocity than any other. It shows up in many ways for leaders:

**Imposing views without careful consideration of others' views.** For example, implementing a change a certain way because they know best and it's always been done that way.

**Unconscious bias.** We all have them; leaders need to regulate them. An unconscious bias is an opinion about someone else, often negative, and usually formed quickly with little evidence. Like the newspaper analogy, people then look for evidence that their initial view is correct, conveniently overlooking the evidence that they may be wrong.

If I hear words like 'always' or 'never', e.g. 'He's always late' or 'She never has anything positive to say', I know immediately that the speaker has an unconscious bias towards the other person. People aren't 'always' or 'never' doing anything.

**Getting even.** When we 'defend the flag at all costs', and someone else appears to 'take a shot', unhealthy conflict ensues. Gossiping, back channel politics, intentional blocking and argument for the sake of it are indicators.

In my experience, this often shows up overtly for men, covertly for women. Both are equally damaging.

If you want to stop a conflict in its tracks, proclaim, 'I think you're right, I've got this wrong!' It will be a very confusing experience for the other party who, fuelled with adrenalin and operating from the emotional brain, will want to continue the conflict while their thinking, rational brain tells them it's over.

So we know that humans need to be right, but how do they decide what to be right about?

# The map is not the territory

When I run this part of my seminar, I start with a simple activity to demonstrate the point. I get the delegates to look out of the window and draw a map of what they can see. They are all looking at the same thing, but the maps are all very different. No map is more or less right than the others, and none of them are 100% accurate because of what is necessarily deleted, distorted or generalised by each person.

Now imagine that each person, wholly convinced of the absolutely correct nature of their map, goes about trying to prove it to the others. They in turn are trying to impose their map on to everyone else. Chaos ensues, and angry chaos at that.

The need to be right about something that is inherently unprovable is absurd, yet we do it all the time.

Put simply, the world is what it is, not how we see it or want it to be. But to make sense of it, we condense it to a scale we can cope with and a meaning that makes sense to us, based on our values, beliefs and outlook on life. Otherwise it would overwhelm us.

These maps, or models of how the world works, are necessary and useful, but they can never do more than approximate the full, real world or the things we see, hear and experience. As in the map drawing activity mentioned above, the actual territory is beyond our comprehension and verbal description. We delete, distort and generalise the world around us. This abstraction simplifies, condenses, symbolises and makes more manageable what is really going on, allowing us to focus on what we think is right and important.

For example, if I walk down the street, I might experience a bank robbery taking place. My perceptions, or the things I record about the event, and the things I don't (deletions) are an abstraction. Someone else witnessing the same event will experience and perceive it differently. The things we think we saw, heard and felt will vary.

Later, when I recount the incident, I might say, 'I saw two robbers, a tall man in his twenties and a blonde woman in her thirties. They ran down the street being chased by two policemen.'

My description gives a sense of what went on, but really it is a loose approximation of what I perceived, which in turn is an approximation of what actually went on. Now there are various maps: mine, the other witness's, the policemen's, the robbers', and that of the person I have told the story to. None of them are the same.

The basis for problems in communication is when we try to impose our map, which by definition isn't full or accurate, upon another person.

If you can appreciate that there are other maps, and that nobody's map is more or less accurate than yours, you can begin to see the world through different eyes and relate to others respectfully and accurately.

---

*The single biggest problem in communication is*
*the illusion that it has taken place.*
**GEORGE BERNARD SHAW**

---

Our maps are created through the gathering of data via the five senses. Our senses highlight aspects of the world and bring those parts to our conscious awareness. We then further filter the data though our values, beliefs and self-made rules. This reinforces those values, beliefs and rules, and sometimes forms new ones. Mostly this happens outside of our conscious awareness, and importantly, most people never realise that values, beliefs and rules can be changed to serve us in better ways.

For example, person A experiences financial hardship early on in life. They hear their parents say things like 'Money doesn't grow on trees' and 'Rich people get that way because they're crooks'. Their map of the world around money and finances will therefore be some-what different to person B, who grew up in financial security where money was perceived as a positive thing to strive for, even though they live in the same 'real world'.

The map of either could change, but will it?

Let's go back to the newspaper analogy. Person A will be more predisposed to read an article criticising a large bonus for a banker and say, 'See, I knew it!'

In the same newspaper, Person B may read an article about recovery in the economy and say, 'See, I knew it!'

Both people are doing what all people do: looking to reinforce and validate their view of the world to such an extent that it becomes an indisputable fact, whereas in reality it's just a firmly held belief.

As a leader, your map and your need to defend it may well be preventing you from holding up the mirror and seeing your true reflection. It allows you to form, maintain and reinforce unconscious negative bias towards others, including people in your team and organisation, preventing the real connection and exquisite communication that must happen to inspire and lead highly engaged and fiercely loyal teams.

You're probably getting parts of it right already; you wouldn't have got to where you are now without doing so. But the ability to be aware of and positively influence our map of the world, while acknowledging and appreciating others' maps, is the top of the mountain of exceptional leadership – the part that's missing when leaders scratch their heads, wondering what else they have to do to get the people bit right in their organisation.

If you start to see others in new lights, you show up as a leader in a different light. People will want to follow you and add to the team, not because you say so, but because they instinctively know you're leading them on a stimulating, compelling journey. Your positive good opinion will feel so incredible that they will constantly live up to or exceed your expectations, and the odd times they come up short, they will move heaven and earth to own and rectify the situation.

You're half way through the book and only just at the end of the first element of the FIERCE Loyalty® model: Focus On Yourself First. If you get this one chapter right, you will need a telescope to look back on where you are today. And if you go first, others will follow.

## KEY ENGAGEMENT AUDIT – LEADERSHIP MAP

What assumptions have you made about the world that hold you back? Pick one - how/when is it untrue?

What assumptions have you made about the people that hold you back? Pick one - how/when is it untrue?

What assumptions have you made about your team that hold you back? Pick one - how/when is it untrue?

If you had to be wrong about one thing, what would it be? How do you know? What would the impact be if you thought differently about that thing?

Go through each team member - what's the one assumption they've made that's holding them back? How could you help them to surface it to think about it?

How could this be an area of dissatisfaction that causes people to leave your organisation? What can you learn from that?

# Small things

Let's do an activity. I want you to imagine that tomorrow, based on this chapter, you decide to make a change that you'll continue to do every day for the next year (365 days). This change could be something as small as:

- Deciding to spend the first fifteen minutes of each day with your team
- Learning a new coaching question daily and trying it out on someone
- Blocking thirty minutes a day in your calendar so you can eat lunch and clear your mind
- Conducting at least one 1:1 per day with a team member.

On Day 2, you choose another small thing that you will also do for the rest of the year (364 days). Then on Day 3, you choose a third small things to do for the rest of the year (363 days). By the last day of the year, you'll be doing 365 small, new things.

But if I asked you to do all 365 new things tomorrow, you probably couldn't because a) you almost certainly wouldn't be able to think of 365 new things to do, and b) it would be impossible to manage.

Question - if the cumulative effect of all those small things was to add up to 100% by the end of the year, what % would each individual change have to be?

Answer - <0.002%.

While I encourage you to strive for big changes, don't forget that small changes over time add up to deliver big results. So my question to you is what will be your 0.002% today?

# Summary

- If you can't lead yourself, you haven't earned the right to lead others

- Stop micromanaging

- You're at least part of the problem

- Treat the source, not the downstream impacts

- Prioritise your team

- Control the emotional hijacks. Take the thirty day test

- You're always role modelling

- Cultivate a positive self-image for yourself and help your team do the same

- You don't need to be right about everything and everyone

- The map is not the territory.

# INSPIRE
# SELF-BELIEF

---

*I have yet to find the man, however exalted his station,*
*who did not do better work and put forth greater effort*
*under a spirit of approval than under a spirit of criticism.*

**CHARLES SCHWAB**

---

What if I told you that you are already sitting on a vast reservoir of talent, creativity, ownership, energy and performance? That you could stop going round in circles trying to fill the motivation and skill gaps in your team yourself and step back while an explosion of talent surfaces to produce results you can only dream of today? And that it can be achieved in a surprisingly short period of time?

I'm always fascinated by the lengths leaders will go to in order to get their teams to perform, all the while overlooking the fundamental human drivers we all share that lead to people wanting to excel and choosing to be the best versions of themselves. And there you have it, the difference between a manager and leader: getting people to the point where they choose excellence.

*Great leaders inspire passion and deliver stellar results through the willing efforts of others.*

Now you've focused on your own effectiveness, the next step to master is the solid foundation upon which everything else is built: inspiring self-belief in others. Once they have it, their talent will come to the fore.

# 'Acres Of Diamonds'

In 1882, Russell Conwell, a Baptist minister from the USA, delivered a lecture: 'Acres Of Diamonds'. It was an engaging and inspiring story, and I've always been struck by the parallels between it and how leaders build and lead their teams. You can find a free copy online if you search for 'Acres of Diamonds'.

To summarise, an African farmer heard that others were making millions by discovering diamond mines. Keen to make his own fortune, he sold his farm to search for himself. He spent the rest of his life searching, unsuccessfully, for the jewels, and died a broken man.

Meanwhile, the farmer he had sold the farm to discovered an unusual stone by a stream that ran through the property. After initially storing it as an intriguing keepsake, he discovered it was in fact one of the largest diamonds ever discovered, and the land he owned was one of the richest diamond mines in the world.

The first farmer had literally owned acres of diamonds, but had sold them for almost nothing to search for them elsewhere. If he had only taken the time to examine his own land carefully, he would have found the riches he sought.

How easily leaders overlook the talent within their own team and give up on trying to turn rough diamonds into precious stones, when all they need is the patience and desire to explore the current landscape.

Don't look without until you have exhausted what's within. You are already sitting on a vast, untapped reservoir of talent, creativity, motivation and energy waiting to be unleashed. To surface it, you just need to get people to believe in themselves, and that's a lot easier than you might think.

The best example of inspiring self-belief I have ever experienced was my leader, Brigid. I joined her team in my late twenties, believing myself to know pretty much everything there was to know. She must have looked at me with a mixture of curiosity and amusement, but it never showed. From the minute I met her to the sad moment I left after five glorious years, I grew immeasurably at a tremendous pace.

I have replicated her approach countless times with my own teams and groups of trainees, and there is always a positive outcome. I'm not even sure she knew she had a method; she just did her thing. And if I'm half the leader she was, I'll be happy.

---

*People who feel appreciated will always do more than what is expected.*

**AMY REES ANDERSON**

---

She understood that from the firm foundation of self-belief, exceptional individuals and teams emerged. You could stretch the edges of a person's capabilities to the very limit, and then a bit beyond, and they would thrive. She knew too that when a person did underperform, they would walk through fire to rectify it, because knowing they hadn't met her expectations, even for a brief period of time, was awful. And the level of loyalty she created was unparalleled.

She understood first and foremost that it is being in 'the combat zone' with one another that holds us back.

Like a star being born, that magical moment where fusion occurs to create a self-sustaining ball of energy and power, the people working for you can get to a point where they too are self-directed, incredible forces. Stunning to watch. Energising to be around.

What Brigid did, and what I now do with consistently positive outcomes, is blindingly simple, yet I've never come across any other leader who uses the same approach. There are four stages:

1. The conscious blindspot

2. Active awareness

3. Reinforcement

4. Adapted style.

Before we review how each stage works, let's consider why it works.

# Releasing human talent

Some of the most powerful human drivers we share with one another throughout our entire lives are to feel respected, valued, appreciated and understood. The great Abraham Maslow, in his well-known Hierarchy Of Needs (1943 paper 'A Theory of Human Motivation'), classifies it under the term 'Esteem'.

From a young age, as we try to get the attention, affection and respect of people around us, our need to feel a sense of worth in the actions and words of others is irresistible. And it's our role models – parents, teachers, close friends and business leaders – who have the biggest impact, be that positive or negative. Role model perceptions are magnified in our minds.

Let's take two children as examples, equal in almost every way: age, sex, intelligence, area they grow up in, parents' affluence, num-ber of siblings, school attended, teachers and so on. Child A struggles in class. He is constantly being told by his parents and teachers that he is lazy and no good. He is compared poorly to his siblings and classmates and rarely gets told anything positive. All in all, he feels pretty worthless. After graduating with below average grades, he ends up with a minimum wage job, struggles to find the motivation to give it his best shot, is reprimanded often, further reinforcing his poor view of himself and the opportunities he has.

---

*People will forget what you said.*
*People will forget what you did. But people will never*
*forget how you made them feel.*

**MAYA ANGELOU**

---

This is a common theme in many people's lives. Is it any wonder that the rate of anxiety, depression and stress related disorders are so prevalent today?

Child B also struggles in class. His parents are worried, and do apply pressure on him to study, but it's explained in a positive way and they support his efforts. They give him praise for good work, and although they tell him when he gets things wrong, they never do it in a way that makes him feel stupid or unwanted. Child B, under a spirit of approval and support, works hard. Although not top in his class, he graduates in the top 15%, which his parents are very proud of. He too gets a level entry job after his education, but he puts forth his best effort. He wants to be successful and knows that he can achieve it if he puts his mind to it. After a few years of diligent work, he gets his first promotion, and so the positive cycle continues.

Both are entirely capable of switching track at any time. Child A could decide to take a more positive approach because he wants to improve his lot; Child B probably wouldn't consciously choose to become more negative, but external circumstances could force a switch of tracks. So why doesn't Child A decide to think, behave and respond in a way that reflects his own sense of self-worth on to himself? Why is he allowing the programming of others to affect him, years later? Three reasons: (a) he doesn't see that his way of behaving - his map of the world - is hindering him; (b) he's not consciously aware of the programming that has occurred over the years, which is now running on auto-pilot and controlling almost every aspect of his life; (c) even if he became aware of it and wanted to change, he wouldn't know how.

Let's recap what we learned in the previous chapter about the leadership map:

1. Be aware you have a map

2. Know you can change your map

3. Choose your thoughts.

Imagine that you are the leader that both Child A and Child B come to work for when they graduate. What immediate impression might you form of both people? Linking back to 'I need to be right about everything and everyone' from the previous chapter, how likely are you to change your initial view of that person? Will you be looking for evidence to support your judgment, or evidence that's contrary to it? Which one might you have a tendency to favour (probably unconsciously)? Which one is more likely to be 'always' or 'never' something?

How people live up to, or rather down to our expectations is exactly how bias forms. And it's how the conditioning of a lifetime, be that positive or negative, is further reinforced. For the most part it happens unconsciously, but the impact is the same.

If your aim is to bring out the best in people and create a culture where everyone can thrive, you, the leader, need to be consciously aware of your bias and operate differently. It's only by people choosing to change, not being told to do so, that they can really improve.

To encourage people to elevate their own level of performance, and sustain it over time, start with the solid foundation of self-belief.

---

*Whether you think you can, or you*
*think you can't - you're right.*

**HENRY FORD**

---

In the motivation game, emotion trumps logic, always. I don't mean having a group hug and sharing stories around an open fire; I mean how you make people feel on a consistent basis. It's simply not enough to give a few words of praise and appreciation in a monthly 1:1, only to be constantly pointing out the negatives or overlooking the positives the rest of the time.

Self-belief sits at the centre of the things you're trying to achieve:

◗ A positive culture of engagement where people grow and flourish

◗ Mutual trust

◗ Healthy task tension where ideas are rigorously debated

◗ Self-motivation, where employees hold themselves to standards higher than you would reasonably expect

◗ A workforce so highly engaged and fiercely loyal to the organisation and the leader that the last thing they're thinking about is leaving.

The benefits to the employee are numerous:

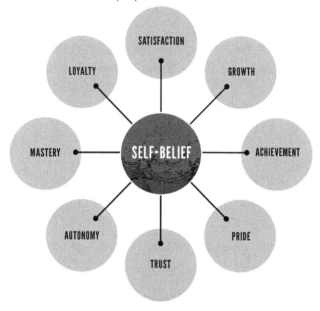

The benefits to the organisation are also numerous:

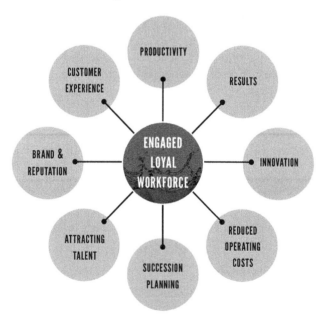

Now let's review each stage of Brigid's approach to inspiring self-belief.

# The conscious blind spot

The following may make you a little uneasy. Trust me, it works.

With the exception of serious issues such as negligence, illegal activity or business risk, for a short period (a few weeks is usually enough), overlook under performance. You don't have to pick people up on every small thing. This creates an impression of safety, preventing people from automatically becoming defensive and keeping them out of the combat zone. After the short period, you can balance the feedback which occurs in the next phase of the model, 'Educate'. This is the only time I break my own rule of not walking past performance, good or bad, without calling it out.

Exercise good judgment here. Mostly, under performance doesn't fall into the serious category, but leaders often react like it does. It's usually just an annoying frustration.

Because this instruction may feel somewhat alarming, before we carry on, do a quick internal audit of your emotional response to it. How's your EQ? What happened in your mind as you considered the idea? Did a particular person or situation come to mind as an obvious example of how it couldn't possibly work? That's the switch that is triggered in our minds when the amygdala, sensing some form of emotional distress or discomfort, starts to override the logical thinking brain.

Of course, this may not have occurred. But if it did, before you move on, you need to regulate your response. This is a great way to develop your EQ in the moment thinking shifts.

Firstly, label what you're feeling and why. Think on that for a few moments. Then call to mind an image of this idea, however alien it is at the moment, having worked in your team. The unconscious mind is unable to distinguish between real events and perceived or imagined ones (the basis of sports psychology).

## Active awareness

During this stage in the model, and beyond, make it a part of your daily activity to look for examples of positive behaviour, however small: an overheard customer call; a creative input in a meeting; a team member staying behind a few minutes after their shift to finish up a query. Also create as many opportunities as possible for more formal observations, e.g. side by side shadowing; observing a presentation; asking stakeholders for feedback. If you're looking for positive behaviour, you'll find it. As quickly as is practical, call it out. Deliver a genuine 'well done' or 'thanks'. It doesn't need to be a big song and dance; the employee just needs to know that you've noticed and appreciated their efforts.

The absence of negative feedback coupled with the focus on positive feedback has a magnifying effect. After a few weeks, people will come to the firm conviction that you value and appreciate them – a powerful experience, especially coming from a role model, which as leader you automatically are. The ensuing sense of personal pride is a cornerstone of self-belief.

## Reinforcement

Whenever you have 1:1s or more formal chats, say again how much you appreciate the positive behaviours you've noticed. As you're establishing trust by showing that you value and appreciate people, reinforcing this is very powerful. Of course the appreciation needs to be genuine, not ticking a box to satisfy a list.

# Adapted style

Look back to the previous chapter where we examined the various communication and working preferences of different people in your teams. In the same way, people like to be appreciated in different ways.

**Commander.** Be direct, to the point, avoid emotional language and point out how the positive behaviour helped to deliver results and performance.

For example: 'Good job on dealing with XYZ task today when others were hesitating. Your decisive actions put us 5% closer to target.'

**Inspirer.** Focus on the creativity you've witnessed and link to other examples of the same thing and the downstream impacts. Inspirers like to see the connection between things.

For example: 'Great idea in the team meeting today. I can't wait to tell Finance, they're going to love how it speeds up the process.'

**Harmoniser.** Be sincere. Let the person know the impact their action had on you personally, and the wider impact on the team.

For example: 'I appreciate how you're always the person who will speak up for the agents. I know the team feel the same.'

**Analyser.** Incorporate specific data and focus on how the Analyser's positive behaviour was efficient and accurate. Analysers prefer praise to be short and in private.

For example: 'Thank you for getting the report to me on time. Smart thinking on the case handling time, it's already showing a 7% efficiency over the week.'

Spend the time, look for the positives. If you're looking for something, you'll see it. Be the leader who calls it out when you're pleased and impressed with your team. It has a profound effect on people.

# KEY ENGAGEMENT AUDIT — RELEASING HUMAN TALENT

If you actively applied the conscious blindspot approach, what's the piece of feedback you could hold off on giving? What impact might that have?

In what ways do you give positive, reinforcing feedback? Reflect back on the past few weeks. What opportunities did you miss to give positive feedback?

Identify one of each of the communication styles in your team or organisation: Commander, Inspirer, Harmoniser and Analyser. How do you know each person has that communication style? Which is closest to your own? How does that influence your working relationship? Which is furthest from your own? How does that influence your working relationship?

If you had to provide positive feedback to each person for the same good piece of work, how would you adapt the content and delivery style to match their communication preference?

How could this be an area of dissatisfaction that causes people to leave your organisation? What can you learn from that?

# Quit defect-managing

The sad truth is that a lot of leaders manage defects rather than drive improvements. They hold a magnifying glass to all errors and demand an explanation. In their quest for unreasonable perfection, they overlook some of the stellar work their reports are producing, and in the ensuing motivation drain, they become a part of the problem.

In the long term, defect-managing is useless. It feels disrespectful to the employees, it undervalues their overall work and the effort they've put forth, and it shows a lack of appreciation and little to no understanding. In short, it violates every basic human driver we all share.

This is not to say underperformance and errors are acceptable, far from it. But to turn things around, you have to turn things around. Focusing just on issues and devaluing people is a large part of the engagement problem. What you want to achieve is an environment where people take pride in and own their tasks and responsibilities and in the main solve their own problems. That is only achieved when people know you believe in them, and they believe in themselves.

The phenomenal book *Turn the Ship Around!* by David Marquet sheds some light on the issue. If you're a leader, or aspire to be one, I cannot recommend it highly enough. In it, he details the remarkable transformation he inspired with the crew on a nuclear submarine. The lessons can be applied anywhere.

---

*We had no need of leadership development programs, the way we ran the ship was the leadership development program.*

**DAVID MARQUET**

---

His chief aim was to turn his passive followers ('Yes, sir, no, sir, whatever you say, sir') into active leaders responsible for their work, at all levels on the ship. I was particularly fascinated by his insights into changing the 'just avoiding errors' culture – or rather, the defect management culture – to one where the entire crew aspired to accomplish something excellent together.

Wow, I love that idea.

Make space for it to be OK to fail, so long as there is learning from it. What would have happened if, after you'd made a few disastrous attempts to walk, your parents had declared, 'You'll never get this right, you're always falling down. I'll carry you from now on'? Can you imagine? How would you have learned if your parents had pointed out how badly you were doing things, then intervened to do them for you? How would you have got better? How would you have accomplished anything? How would you feel the sense of pride that comes from owning a task you have mastered, even if at the beginning you weren't perfect?

## KEY ENGAGEMENT AUDIT – QUIT DEFECT MANAGING

In what ways are you focusing too much on the wrong problems/errors? In what ways do you focus on the right problems/errors? How does this drive ownership and performance improvement?

How could this be an area of dissatisfaction that causes people to leave your organisation? What can you learn from that?

# The language of improvement

When you sit on a train, you can either face in the direction of travel, or away from it. The train is going the same way regardless, but your focus is different.

With teams, when we set goals and directions, it's the same thing. We can either focus on moving towards something, e.g. becoming the Number 1 team for quality, or away from something, e.g. getting out of the bottom quartile for making errors. On the surface, they may seem to achieve the same thing, but where each one directs your attention makes a big difference.

A personal example could be that I want to run 5km in under thirty mins (a towards goal) versus I don't want to be overweight and unfit (an away from goal). One focuses on the positive improvement to be gained, the other on the negative to be lost. Both are two sides of the same coin.

---

*Whatever you consistently think*
*about and focus upon you move toward.*

**TONY ROBBINS**

---

Your unconscious mind is an excellent provider of things/experiences/outcomes. It assumes that if you're thinking about something a lot, especially when you add emotional intensity, you must want more of that thing. It then works to bring that about through your actions and decisions, even if you're thinking about a negative outcome. The unconscious mind makes no value judgment, it just delivers.

Importantly, the unconscious mind also deletes negatives. For example, if I asked you not to think of a blue elephant, you'd have to think of it first in order not to think of it. The more you try, the harder it gets. So if you are constantly thinking, 'I don't want to be overweight', your unconscious takes this to mean 'I want to be overweight', because it can't process the negative. Your conscious mind can, but your motivation to act and your decisions, e.g. to go to the gym or not to eat that cake, won't reside in the conscious mind.

The best metaphor I've come across on this subject is from the late, great Earl Nightingale. He parallels this situation to planting seeds in a field, the fertile field being the unconscious mind, the farmer being the conscious mind. The farmer can choose to plant anything s/he wants: corn, wheat, or deadly nightshade; the field will return the crop just as plentifully regardless.

So, if I predominantly focus my thoughts on, or 'plant', running 5km, my unconscious mind will adjust my desire, action, choices and motivation to that. If I inadvertently plant 'I want to be overweight', then my desire, action, choices and motivation will support that.

Think about that for a moment. It's so simplistic, it's almost unbelievable. The things that predominantly play on the internal screen of your mind act as a signal to your unconscious that you want more of them. I firmly believe that this should be taught at school.

When I first came across this notion many years ago, I dismissed it initially. It seemed almost absurd. But once I'd studied, understood, embraced and adopted the notion, my life changed in so many incredible ways. Among other things, the dive centre I ran in Thailand came about by my use of this information.

Let's use a different analogy. Think of your mind like a restaurant.

**Customer = conscious mind**. The conscious mind accounts for approximately 10% of your mind's activity. It is the thinking part of your mind, aware of the present moment. Taking information from the outside world through the five senses, it can mentally visualise and create things you've never experienced before and perceive the difference between the real world and the imagined internal world and memory. It has the ability to either accept or reject outside ideas, e.g. something you may see on the TV news, or hear in a conversation.

**Menu = consciously perceived (but not in reality) full potential.**

**Waiter = subconscious mind**. The subconscious mind accounts for approximately 50-60% of the brain's capabilities. It stores accessible information and deals with recent or habitual memories.

Have you ever experienced a time when you've driven part way home and suddenly thought, Wow, how did I get here? For a short spell you were on auto-pilot. The subconscious mind knew the way and how to drive and didn't need the direction of the conscious mind. If a police siren had sounded or car horn blared out, your conscious mind would immediately have taken over again to assess the current situation and any threat it may pose.

**Chef = unconscious mind**. The unconscious mind accounts for the remaining 30-40% of brain activity. It stores all memories and past experiences. Everthing that we experience, right back to childhood, is evaluated and then recorded in the unconscious mind. It's from these memories and experiences, particularly those from our early lives, that our beliefs, habits and behaviours are formed to give us our map of the world. It's why our maps can be so hidden to us; the things and events upon which the 'lessons' about life are learned are forgotten, leaving us with just the invisible behaviour patterns that result.

The unconscious communicates to the conscious through feelings, emotions, ,sensations and dreams. It also directs behaviour, actions and decisions. Simply stated, it's in charge.

In our analogy, the waiter would have to show the chef a picture (or symbol) of the order, as it does not operate with language, which is a relatively new form of communication in evolutionary terms. That's why the images held on the screen of your mind are so important, it's the way your unconscious determines what to focus on and how the direct your behaviour. Importantly, unlike the conscious mind, it cannot reject ideas impressed upon it. It simply accepts them as the truth.

**Kitchen = true potential.** The full storehouse of ingredients needed to make almost any recipe imaginable. Out of sight of the 'customer', the conscious mind, it is there nonetheless.

The customer reviews the menu, the waiter takes the order, then passes it back to the chef, who has all of the ingredients in the kitchen and makes the action happen. The chef cooks up what s/he's been asked for, then sends it back to be enjoyed. S/he never questions the order – s/he is unable to. S/he simply serves up what's asked for, even though s/he has the potential to make thousands of different and better recipes (outcomes).

This is quite a simplistic explanation. If you're interested to have a deeper understanding, I recommend you research Neuro Linguistic Programming (NLP).

---

*What you think about, you bring about.*
**BOB PROCTOR**

---

If you or your organisation constantly prioritises avoiding errors, even though your conscious intention is to get less of that thing/result/ outcome, errors are what you focus on. Therefore you are more likely to bring them about than reduce them.

Do yourself and your team a favour: spend more time focusing on what you do want, e.g. the successful outcomes you want to achieve, the recognition you want to get, and less time simply picking up the pieces of defects.

- We have to reduce quality errors vs we want to become the best team for quality scores

- We must reduce attrition vs we want to have to highest tenure and internal promotions

- We need to stop overspending on the travel budget vs we want to become the most financially efficient department

- We have to reduce customer complaints vs we want to achieve the best customer loyalty scores in the business.

Let the team guide the 'how'.

## KEY ENGAGEMENT AUDIT – THE LANGUAGE OF IMPROVEMENT

Consider the team/individual goals you've set. In what ways are they 'away from' goals? How has this limited success? How could they be adapted to be 'towards' goals? Which are already 'towards' goals? What could you teach others about effective goal setting?

How could this be an area of dissatisfaction that causes people to leave your organisation? What can you learn from that?

# Play to strengths

At this critical stage, the focus is all on the positive. Even if there is a long way to travel for the employee, a good leader starts with highlighting the positives, thus building trust and confidence and steering out of the combat zone. Later, when the foundation is firm, you can deliver any message and it will land properly, because the employee won't feel under attack.

> *Leave everyone you meet with*
> *an impression of increase.*
> **WALLACE WATTLES,**
> **THE SCIENCE OF GETTING RICH**

In addition, there is only so much improvement to be made in a person's development areas. But there is no limit to the improvements that can be made in an existing area of strength. Obviously people need thresholds and effective levels of competence in job specific skills, but once they've achieved these, switch track to developing and harnessing their strengths. This is especially useful when driving engagement.

A more formal way to do this, in addition to the informal method of catching the employee doing something right in the moment, is to introduce a programme to surface key skills and strengths so they can be identified and reinforced. Again, when the foundation is firm you can switch to focus on development areas. But not yet. My personal favourite programme is **Clifton StrengthsFinder™ 2.0**. There are others on the market, but I find the richness and accuracy of the reporting in this one to be outstanding.

Here's how you can use it successfully with teams.

- Buy the *StrengthsFinder* book, one per team member as their unique online assessment access code is contained within the book
- Get the team to complete the online assessment
- Facilitate a team workshop to review the results: what were the similarities and shared strengths in the team? What were the outliers? Etc.
- Review an upcoming project or team assignment
- As a group, decide what strengths are needed for the successful completion and implementation of the project, e.g. Analytical, Communication, Harmony, Strategic, etc.
- Plot the desired strengths against those within the team, and assign tasks based on strengths.

This is not only a highly engaging and rewarding activity for the team (team cohesion), it gives you the precious opportunity to praise and give positive feedback around their skills. The employees then know you value and appreciate them (individual engagement), and the project is completed to a high standard with enthusiasm and passion (business performance).

This time, when you are focusing on positives and temporarily sidestepping under performance, can be frustrating. What's so hard in just doing your job, right? In an ideal world, you're 100% right. Meanwhile, back in the real world, you aren't.

---

*People do the best they can with what they've got.*

---

A great perspective I learned from a phenomenal leader, **Michele McNickle Driver**, is to believe that people do things with positive intentions, even if sometimes there is a negative outcome. Nobody sits in a dark room, plotting how to make your life miserable; nobody intentionally drops the ball to see the wave of frustration roll across your face. People don't underperform just to see how you'll deal with it this time.

Using this lens takes any potential frustration down a notch so you can focus on the positives. It's another great way to develop your EQ as you immediately become aware of frustrations growing and change your thoughts in the moment.

## KEY ENGAGEMENT AUDIT – PLAY TO STRENGTHS

Have you surfaced and documented individual strengths within your team? Have you allocated tasks and responsibilities based on strengths? How could you implement a strengths-based assessment tool with your team?

How could this be an area of dissatisfaction that causes people to leave your organisation? What can you learn from that?

# The boundaries of accomplishment

In the chapter 'Focus On Yourself First', I introduced Maxwell Maltz's concept of psycho-cybernetic mechanisms. This is the thermostat in your mind, fixed firmly in your blueprint of who you are and what you can accomplish. It prevents you from falling below a certain level of accomplishment, which is good, but also sets a ceiling above which you won't rise, which is negative.

This chapter has been about helping others to raise their upper threshold; to break free from the limitations that others planted in their minds about who they could be and what they could achieve.

Solid self-belief, especially that which is given to us by important role models in our lives, is a powerful force. It may take a little time to unstitch the thinking from the past, so be patient. At the heart of all of us is someone who wants to feel secure and confident. We all need to think highly of ourselves, not in a conceited way, but in a strong, healthy way.

As a leader, you are in a unique and remarkable position to be a guiding light to someone else. In doing so, not only will you grow yourself, but you will help to unleash untold potential in them. And when they reach their point of 'fusion' where the energy they're generating is tangible, they cannot help but become stars. Then you sit back and watch their creative force in awe, just as Brigid did for me, and as I have tried to pay forwards every opportunity I can. The ripple effect of one outstanding leader is astonishing.

The final vital component of building rock solid self-belief is at a team level (team cohesion). You must take every opportunity to showcase the excellent work of your team. Copy the wider leadership team into emails about positive performance, distribute customer feedback, and so on. If you're doing this to some extent already, are there opportunities to do it more? Can you inspire others to do the same? At this stage of inspiring self-belief, it is essential that you're a cheerleader for your team as often and as widely as you can be.

When your team members know you not only appreciate them, but you're proud of them and their achievements, their performance and engagement will explode on the self-belief this generates. As with all of the stages of this model, your appreciation must be authentic, not a tick in a box which they will see through straight away.

It's around this stage that you will start to see the green shoots appearing. You may notice:

- A happier vibe and good energy about the office/workplace
- More positive communication
- More creativity and innovation as people start to feel good about themselves
- Solutions to problems
- Levels of proactivity and productivity rise
- Management conversations go down (about lateness, attitude etc.) as leadership conversations increase
- Discretionary effort increases where people go over and above without having to be asked - a major indication of engagement and loyalty.

# Summary

⭕ With solid self-belief, people can reach their true potential

⭕ Basic human drivers are to feel respected, valued, appreciated and understood

⭕ Cultivate a conscious blindspot and focus on positives

⭕ Deliver positive feedback in a style that suits the other person

⭕ Stop managing defects

⭕ Play to strengths

⭕ Believe in positive intentions, even if there are negative outcomes

⭕ Be the team's cheerleader.

# EDUCATE

---

*Education does not mean teaching people what they do not know. It means teaching them to behave as they do not behave.*

**JOHN RUSKIN**

---

What if one well-placed and powerful instruction was the key to unlocking someone's potential? What if we could tap into the way all humans learn to make progress and growth a rewarding experience that people look forward to in work? Now there is a firm foundation of self-belief, what if people welcomed and sought constructive feedback in the spirit it's intended and acted upon it?

Once people believe in themselves, and believe you believe in them, you can up the pace of learning and experience to astonishing levels.

The key is absolute clarity on what you expect and constant reinforcement of those expectations.

## Look to the horizon

Some years ago, I travelled around the world on my own. I could fill a book with the things I learned about myself and the world during that year, but one lesson nicely describes this Educate part of the model.

I spent a few weeks in British Columbia, Canada. What an incredible part of the world it is – the people are so friendly and the scenery is breathtaking. While I was in Whistler, I decided I would learn to ski. It was May, the final few weeks of the ski season, and the snow on the lower slopes had melted. Ordinarily, beginners would learn on the gentler slops, but it wasn't possible, so my instructor and I headed to the top of what seemed like Everest.

I didn't take to it all that quickly, mainly because I was terrified I would fall down the side of the mountain. Not to be beaten, I persevered, but after three days, I was still like a newborn giraffe. It wasn't pretty. I shook with the effort it took to ski down a mountain in plough position. My legs were like jelly, my ego was torn. Maybe skiing was just beyond me.

On the fourth day, I had a new instructor – I secretly think the previous one had lost the will to live trying to teach me. We took one slow pass down the mountain, and I was ready to give up. Just before we set off again, she gave me a simple enough instruction and checked that I understood what she'd said.

'Stop looking at your feet, look at the horizon.'

Not look at my feet? I thought. But how will they know what to do?

So we set off, and soon enough I was looking at my feet, willing them to do the right thing. The instructor reminded me to look at the horizon, and in seconds, two astonishing things happened. Firstly, I was overwhelmed at the beauty of the scene around me: one of nature's jewels. Then, my feet, that hadn't needed my visual control to do what feet do, instinctively started skiing. And not the awkward plough skiing of before, but parallel turn skiing.

My instructor saw the source of my problem and knew the simple instruction needed to unlock my potential. She didn't need to micro-manage the process for me; through her substantial experience, she was able to educate me about the thing that was getting in my way and hold me to her instruction, allowing learning and achievement to flow from it.

This is a great example of educating: the leader uses their considerable knowledge and experience to issue specific potential-unlocking instructions, demands compliance (for the benefit of the individual), then allows the person to execute the instruction and feedback on progress or remaining challenges. This is the basis of all human growth.

By having a clear idea of where I was going, I found the skills and behaviours necessary to get there unconsciously surfaced. Was I an Olympic skier? No (although with practice, who knows?). Was I significantly better than I had been? Yes. Not only that, I was enjoying it.

Let's consider why this stage is so powerful.

The skills and behaviours for this chapter speak to another basic human driver: the need to get better at things. It's why we learn to walk, even though we fall over 1,000 times and bump our heads. It explains the notion of hobbies. There's no monetary reward for playing the guitar, or gymnastics, horse riding, gliding, tennis, learning languages; the intrinsic value is in getting better at your hobby, mastering it and enjoying the fruits of your labour.

---

*We like to get better at stuff.*

**DAN PINK**

---

Once people feel secure about your view of them (Inspire Self-belief), you can help them to feel good about what they're doing. Not just by praising them, but by helping them to get even better at it, which satisfies this human driver. By moving on from focusing only on the positives to helping people improve in areas of development, you can begin the real business of leadership.

# What is education?

Education is helping people to get better at things by learning and mastering new skills.

I put education into four buckets:

1. Knowledge - e.g. how do I enter customer details on to the system?

2. Skill - e.g. how do I ask the customer for those details so they willingly share them?

3. Behaviour - e.g. how do I ensure I record all details accurately, 100% of the time?

4. Attitude - e.g. why should I care about it? Why should it matter to me to get it right?

Phases 1 and 2 are relatively straightforward. The knowledge and skill of a job can be taught in training sessions and practised until mastered. There tends to be an upper threshold - there is only ever so much knowledge to learn about a role.

Phases 3 and 4 are ongoing, can always be improved, and responsibility to own these phases sits firmly with the employee. The path of emotional intelligence and exquisite communication that Brigid showed to me became a lifelong pursuit of excellence, and long may it continue, but she could only illuminate the path. It was mine to walk.

Contrary to popular belief, you cannot motivate another person. The choice is an internal one. You can only create an environment and culture where they are more likely to choose to be motivated. This is precisely why cultures of engagement are so compelling. People who are engaged *do* choose to be motivated.

The 'what', 'how' and 'who' of education depends in the main on the other party. This phase does not look the same for everyone; it depends on some variables:

- Their level of experience and tenure
- Complexity of their role
- Their confidence levels
- Their desire to progress
- Where they are now in terms of attitude
- Their preferred communication style.

I've led some amazing teams over the years. Some were small, just two people; some were large. Some were well established; some I set up from scratch. Some were initially underperforming; some were already rock stars. Some were glad I was there; some weren't. No matter the starting point, I led them all to excellent performance and generated fierce loyalty, none more so than the team I built and led in 2013. (I've changed team members' names to protect their identities.)

The Learning and Development function was new in this organisation, and my appointment was the first piece of the puzzle. A few months later, when the strategy was clearer, I appointed four new trainers to fill the team. Two were internal movers who knew a lot about the company's industry and its processes, but were new to training as a profession; two were external hires, both experienced trainers but new to the industry.

The first phase, Inspire Self-belief, began the moment they started: four fresh-faced and eager people, each with their own unique set of hopes, aspirations, experience, attitudes and fears.

I held them in the highest possible regard. Their development, helping them reach their full potential, was my fulltime occupation as their leader, be that through praising their positive behaviours (Inspire

Self-Belief), introducing them to and role modelling even better ways (Educate), or not shying away from highlighting under performance (more on that in `Raise the Bar`).

In the first two months, I orchestrated as many opportunities as I could to provide positive feedback. In addition to the impromptu opportunities I found and called out in the moment, I held daily informal huddles where I made sure to call them out again to the whole team. I held ad hoc meetings weekly to review tasks and progress, again using the time to reinforce what I was happy about.

For the two experienced trainers, I observed all of their training sessions in the first few months to provide powerful positive feedback with small amounts of developmental feedback. For the two new trainers, I allowed them to observe me presenting first of all so they had a starting point, then we deconstructed my presentation and they gave me feedback, which I gratefully received. Gradually I passed it over to them to deliver parts of programmes so they learned the craft safely, and received feedback along the way.

**Emma** was an experienced soft skills trainer e.g. communication skills. I hired her externally because of the existing learning and development skill she brought, knowing she would hit the floor running and add value from the start. She had a strong presence in and out of the training room, was very focused and professional, and her attention to detail was incredible. She always thoroughly researched her training topics, met deadlines and was logical and precise.

Initially, she preferred to work on assignments alone, not because she was anti-social, but because she liked things to be done in a certain way. Opening up to the rest of the team for support and asking for help was not that easy for Emma.

The `look at the horizon` education gap for her was to be willing to collaborate. Through collaboration, we all achieve more.

**Lisa** was also an experienced trainer, although her background was more towards the technical training side of things. She was very open and bubbly, although it seemed to me she was desperately lacking in confidence and self-belief (she later admitted that a pervious boss had bullied her and undermined her at every turn, so no wonder). Her lack of confidence initially led to a lot of questioning and self-doubt, and high dependence on me to confirm she was on the right track with things, but she formed natural easy relationships with people at all levels, and her warm personality shone through and established trust.

The 'look at the horizon' education gap for her was that she wouldn't be in the team if I didn't trust her judgment. It's OK to fail, just as long as you learn.

**Helen** was a smart, poised, graceful and humble individual. I appointed her from within the company and she was a popular choice. Her knowledge of the policies and processes was remarkable - perfect for new hire training. She was a keen student in the art of classroom management, having no previous experience as a trainer, and she took all feedback gratefully. As a reflector, she took her time to examine things from all angles, and her contributions to discussions were always well-considered and useful. It did come across at times, however, that she either couldn't or wouldn't join in debate and discussion. She also lacked the presence and gravitas to manage large groups of learners.

The 'look at the horizon' education gap for her was to bring her thoughts and opinions to the team and be prepared to debate ideas.

**Sue** was an engaging and charismatic ball of energy. She had a big personality, and wasn't afraid to use it, injecting humour and energy into meetings and training events. She wasn't the most thorough or detail-oriented person, instead relying on her verbal fluency and in-the-moment creativity to see her through, but she eagerly took on assignments and was quick to complete them. What held Sue back the most was that her eagerness was often taken as bluntness and domination, especially in team meetings, and her lack of attention to detail was not appreciated by her stakeholders.

The 'look at the horizon' education gap for her was to be willing to be vulnerable, humble and authentic. There had to be trust in order for her to be a part of the team.

To summarise:

| EMMA | LISA | HELEN | SUE |
|------|------|-------|-----|
| **HELPING** | **HELPING** | **HELPING** | **HELPING** |
| Professional, attention to detail, logical, precise, met deadlines | Established quick and easy relationships, bubbly, built trust | Authentic, humble, took time to reflect for insight | Energetic, enthusiastic, creative, lively, had presence |
| **HINDERING** | **HINDERING** | **HINDERING** | **HINDERING** |
| Not perceived as a team player | Lacked confidence and self-belief | Quiet, reflective nature lacked gravitas | Overbearing and overpowering |

The Educate phase started when I was sure they had rock solid self-belief about themselves and my view of them:

- I clearly communicated their 'look to the horizon' development area and my expectation on improvement

- I was alert for any opportunity to help them individually identify and overcome their main limiting behaviour and beliefs

- I switched away from just giving positive feedback to provide more balanced feedback

- **O** I put responsibility on to them to identify and own the resolution for gaps in their knowledge and skill

- **O** I provided less and less solutions, instead coaching them to generate their own

- **O** I stopped leading the weekly team meeting, instead having an even mixture of contributors

- **O** I implemented a programme of learning that allowed them to grow as people and have compelling and rich trainer led discussions, e.g. stages of team development, emotional intelligence, storytelling and metaphor in learning

- **O** I moved from focusing on strengths to surfacing development areas

- **O** We got clear on goals, mine and theirs.

---

## KEY ENGAGEMENT AUDIT – LOOK TO THE HORIZON

What's the one thing each of your reports needs to master to achieve the biggest leap in performance and behaviour? Knowing it's for their ultimate benefit, how will you demand improvement in this area in a way that invites ownership and accountability?

How could this be an area of dissatisfaction that causes people to leave your organisation? What can you learn from that?

---

# Crystal clear goals

If you help people to get clear on the goals you have for them and the goals they need to have for themselves, they will have a compelling track to run on. Their inner resource and potential can surface and come to bear. It's the difference between potential and kinetic energy.

**Your goals.** At this stage, set goals that are a small stretch from where people are currently, but are still compelling and worthwhile. They represent improvement, not risk of failure, or if there is risk, it's not in an area fundamental to performance, where failure would significantly dent people's confidence.

**Their goals.** This is the time to introduce teams members' ownership for their development, and setting their own goals is a vital part of this. Questions that can elicit their creative answers include:

- What's the main goal you're focused on at the moment?
- What tells you that's the priority?
- What would success look like?
- Three months from now, what would make you most proud?
- What difference would this make to you?
- When have you faced a similar situation?
- Who could you speak to?

Their goals also provide a perfect opportunity for positive reinforcement, e.g. when they do something right that takes them a step closer to their goal.

## Adaptive communication

The final element of Education is how it is communicated. Subtle adaptations in how you communicate with individuals will affect how the message lands with them.

Let's use my former team as an example.

| EMMA: ANALYSER | LISA: INSPIRER | HELEN: HARMONISER | SUE: COMMANDER |
|---|---|---|---|
| Professional, attention to detail, logical, precise, met deadlines | Established quick and easy relationships, bubbly, built trust | Authentic, humble, took time to reflect for insight | Energetic, enthusiastic, creative, lively, had presence |
| **MY COMMUNICATION APPROACH** | **MY COMMUNICATION APPROACH** | **MY COMMUNICATION APPROACH** | **MY COMMUNICATION APPROACH** |
| Sent agendas ahead of time; made logical, sequential plans; made written record of discussions; agreed completion deadlines and focused on timescales and smaller chunks of measurable improvement | Had more impromptu and informal meetings as and when needed; started discussions with rapport building; sat next to Lisa in the office; linked to long term objectives and sense of future aspirations | Issued key topics ahead of team meetings for initial reflection time; in 1:1s asked Helen to think of solutions and come back to me later in the day; linked individual performance to overall team performance | Quick daily check-ins to reconnect on progress towards deadlines; formal 1:1s, short and standing up; direct discussions; came straight to the point with feedback and development areas |

My willingness and ability to alter my communication approaches slightly got me on to each person's wavelength. You don't need to make big changes to see big differences.

# Storytelling

Humans have spent thousands of years communicating with one another through stories. They are compelling, engaging and lead to that 'Aha, I see what you mean' moment.

Teaching new knowledge and skills, sharing a vision, and setting goals that 'look to the horizon' are powerful tools in the leader's toolkit.

From stories (such as my ski story) to analogies (such as the map is not the territory), the Educate phase is enriched by your ability to use parallels to make sense of your key points.

There are many useful and important books and videos available on the subject, e.g. the TED talks. If you're not already a storyteller, I recommend you invest some time in becoming one.

Using these steps, I could see my team members growing in front of my eyes, and so could the wider organisation. It was amazing. They had an air about them. Something about the way they conducted themselves, how they spoke to each other and others in the organisation, the contributions they made in meetings, how they fulfilled their promises to the highest standard, even how they dressed said they were showing up at full strength. And the most telling indication of all, on top of the fabulous feedback I was receiving from people in other departments, was their discretionary effort. What a remarkable team. And we hadn't even finished cycling through the model - they arrived at this point half way through it and got even better.

## KEY ENGAGEMENT AUDIT – CRYSTAL CLEAR GOALS

Do you document goals for your reports? Are they a combination of your goals for them and their own?

In what ways do the goals you and your team set drive engagement? In what ways do they detract from engagement? As a leader of leaders, how do you ensure that this is replicated throughout your division?

How could this be an area of dissatisfaction that causes people to leave your organisation? What can you learn from that?

# Landing group education

Sometimes, the thing holding the team back is the team itself.

Some years ago, I was appointed as the Training and Quality Manager for a finance company. The team had an outstanding relationship with the outgoing role-holder and some team members did not take well to my appointment.

The first few weeks were challenging. Half of the team members were OK with the change. The others were not, and they weren't afraid to show it. However, I understood why they were responding so emotionally. They'd had a strong working relationship with the previous leader, and the old set-up was known and comfortable. I was more demanding and expected greater effort and results, but allowed them a little leeway to get to grips with the new world.

After a couple of weeks, I knew one or two of them were stuck, and they were dragging the team down with them. The time for considering the individuals was over; the time to consider the wider team had begun. The gloves can come off at this stage; you no longer need to protect people from their egos.

In the next team meeting, I reviewed the change curve (shock, denial, fear, anger, resistance, acceptance, openness, integration) as part of the standing team development agenda item. Using recent events, I illustrated the learning, creating awareness and shining a light on the issue. After the learning, I raised the possibility that those who were in my view wilfully stuck at the anger phase were harming the team, and if they felt they were unable to move past their emotional response to losing the previous leader, regrettably, that I would have no choice but to remove them from the team. I mentioned no names, I pointed no fingers. I didn't need to. Everyone knew who they were, most especially those individuals.

Almost immediately, their behaviour changed. I anticipated as much. I had made them uncomfortable, and it didn't feel good.

They were a bit sheepish to begin with, unsure of where they stood and lacking the all-important self-belief. Keen to reinforce positive new behaviours, an important aspect of the Educate phase, I showed my recognition and appreciation of their positive behaviours and attitudes. They knew immediately that I wasn't harbouring any sort of ill will.

The team went on to drive significant improvements in quality, start a coaching and development culture when delivering feedback, create a new rewards system to call out and recognise outstanding quality within the centre, and become highly productive and effective. They became one of the most effective teams I ever led.

The key? Don't mess about at this stage; tell it as it is. I absolutely meant it when I said I would take people out of the team if they couldn't or wouldn't improve their behaviour. It's not your job to make it easy; it's to make it possible and compelling. People need to know that *they* own their performance and behaviour, not you.

---

## KEY ENGAGEMENT AUDIT – LANDING GROUP EDUCATION

What element of team behaviour needs to be surfaced and improved in order to drive performance, morale and engagement? What plan do you have to achieve that?

How could this be an area of dissatisfaction that causes people to leave your organisation? What can you learn from that?

# Summary

- Getting better at stuff feels good; it's a basic human driver

- One size fits no one

- Meet people where they are

- Balance the feedback – positive and developmental

- Pass responsibility for people's goals to them

- Look at the horizon to unlock potential

- Adapt your communication style to the individual

- Tell great stories

- Feedback on team effectiveness for the greater good of all.

# RAISE THE BAR

---

*Go as far as you can see; when you get there,*
*you'll be able to see further.*

**THOMAS CARLYLE**

---

What if you now had a rock solid platform that you could stand on to stretch your people to the very edges of their capability? What if they loved the journey, and with each passing day became more energised, engaged and effective? What if you could watch their quantum leaps in performance with amazement?

The previous stages of the model: Focus On Yourself First, Inspire Self-belief and Educate were predominantly driven by you. From this point on the driving force will be your team members. Raise The Bar is the stage where you pass the baton of ownership and momentum firmly to them.

## Quantum leaps

It's time to up the ante. The transitions into this phase may seem smooth, but the gear shifts will be significant. They must be.

Let's recap where we are. We've focused on positive feedback and reinforcement for a short spell to encourage solid self-belief. We then entered the Educate phase, balancing the feedback and being clear about our expectations, carefully pushing people to enjoy getting better at their jobs.

If 'getting better at stuff' feels good, being stretched to the very edges of your capability and comfort is exhilarating. In the wonderful words of **Price Pritchett**, it 'results in explosive jumps in performance that put you far beyond the next logical step'.

At this stage, Raise The Bar, you are introducing elements of risk to people. There is something big to play for, and something big to lose. It requires people to show up to succeed, and by this stage, with their solid confidence in their abilities and your view of them, they are eager and willing, if a little cautious to begin with.

People will arrive here at different times. Like all stages of the model, the time needs to be right for the individual, but when the time is right and you shift gears on what you expect of them, they elevate rapidly in terms of the level they operate at, the tasks they undertake and their personal excellence. This is the phase where you hand over responsibility for them to lead themselves. It concludes in the final stage of the model, Empower, but you lay the seeds for it down here.

The specific focus areas in which to raise the bar are:

The most remarkable part of the Raise The Bar stage is how people grow. They mature, if you like. Their personal pride is so high it shines out of them. I don't have children myself, but I can imagine there is a moment in every parent's life where they realise that their son or daughter has reached adulthood. In this one regard, I can imagine the moment is similar for a leader.

It's likely you will be astonished at the levels of creativity, productivity and performance achieved during this stage. So will your team. The bonds between you will tighten. An unspoken alliance will exist. Everyone will be pulling their weight, not adding to issues, and acting with shared enthusiasm for the achievement of individual and team goals.

Naturally, some people are there from the start, but mostly, in my experience, they are not. I can't remember that specific moment for me when I was working with Brigid, but then I wasn't looking out for it. To me it was a fluid journey, but I bet she saw it, just as I've seen it with my teams. After Brigid led me through this stage, I was on fire. I had become the star I'd mistakenly thought I was when I joined Brigid's team. I was hyper-engaged and fiercely loyal.

I took approximately four months from joining Brigid's team to be ready for us to start this Raise The Bar phase. As we journeyed through the model, we took less and less time in each phase, because I was operating at a higher level, my relationship with Brigid was solid, and I was actively looking for opportunities to improve.

---

## KEY ENGAGEMENT AUDIT — QUANTUM LEAPS

Who in your team or organisation is ready now for a big jump in responsibility or the tasks they undertake? How do you know? What has held you back from doing that so far?

How could this be an area of dissatisfaction that causes people to leave your organisation? What can you learn from that?

---

# Feedback

In the Raise The Bar stage, you no longer need to create 'sand pit' safe environments. You can stretch people to their maximum, and it starts with the feedback you provide.

The essential element to this is you can feedback anything to anyone, providing the intention is positive. If you just want to unload both barrels, don't. If you want to show people trust and respect, and provide a transparent platform for them to learn and grow, tell them what they need (maybe not want) to hear. It's one of the most fundamental responsibilities of a leader. Not to do so, to shy away from it in any way, is to abandon your duties.

In the opening chapter, I mentioned the worst feedback I ever received, and why it turned out to be the best. It was from Brigid, the most influential role model leader I ever had, and was a critical turning point that later defined my life.

When I joined Brigid's team, I was arrogant and convinced of my own superior talents. I was completely unaware that when less expe- rience team members gave me constructive feedback on my training delivery, I was defensive, rude and unprofessional. Who did they think they were? In every other regard, I was a top performer, and Brigid could have just looked the other way on this one issue that was in my blind spot, as all of my previous leaders must have done. But she didn't. She had the courage, trust and respect to reflect it back to me in a way that was neither sugar coated (believe me, I still go red when I think about it), nor was it aggressive or accusatory. She stuck to the facts: the things she had seen, heard and experienced. It was twenty years ago, so I don't recall the words exactly, but it was along the lines of how I had embarrassed her, the team and myself with my unprofessional behaviour, and that it was completely unacceptable if I wanted to stay in the team.

It did not feel good!

She didn't have to tell me to change - I would have walked through fire to resolve it, and I did. To this day, I can trace back most of my key relationship skills, emotional intelligence and humility to that one critical moment in my life.

Thank goodness she told me. But if she had told me in my first few weeks (I bet she wanted to), before we were on a sure footing, I may well have dismissed it, or entered the combat zone with her with my defences up. I may have externally altered my behaviour, but it would still have been simmering under the surface, preventing me from reaching my full potential.

She gave it to me straight. It stung. I changed.

## Courageous conversations

The ability to deliver a tough message that lands in the right way doesn't come easily to a lot of leaders. If they are Harmonisers, they fear it will upset and offend people and they sugar coat it so much that it's awkward or has no impact, or they may avoid it altogether. The more direct Commander types can forget they are dealing with human beings and deliver it so bluntly that it's rude and offensive and leads to confrontation. Neither way achieves anything long lasting.

There is a different way: a way that maintains and even builds trust; a way that, although not easy, is manageable; a way that highlights underperformance or poor behaviours while getting the person to own them, accept them and change them.

The points below may help you to see the nature and purpose of the message in a different light, removing any mental barriers and allowing your own skill and talent to rise to the surface.

**It's not your job to make it easy.** It's your job to tell the truth.

**Coach the behaviour, not the whole person.** Have specific examples of what you've seen, heard and experienced.

**Don't generalise.** For example, instead of saying, 'You're always late' or 'You're always negative', say, 'You've been late four times this month' or 'When I told the team xxx in the meeting yesterday, your response was yyy which had a negative effect.'

**Be the person who gives the positive messages too.** You have to earn the right to give difficult messages. Nobody wants to hear just bad feedback. That is why the Inspire Self-belief and Educate phases are so critical.

**Anticipate a possible emotional reaction.** It's natural. Be the leader if it happens, and do not join person there. Instead, role model the behaviour you expect by not provoking the situation, e.g. think about the volume of your voice; avoid sarcasm; don't interrupt; pause the meeting for five minutes if they need to compose themselves.

**Use empathy to take excuses off the table.** For example, counter, 'I'm not the only person who is late, why are you focusing on me?' with 'It's true that sometimes other people are late. I'm speaking to you about it because it happens more frequently/is having a bigger impact', or 'If I don't agree, I feel I should be able to say it. I'm not at school' with 'I do value the fact that you raise concerns others may not feel comfortable about saying. So that we can both have a constructive discussion about it, I need you to present a solution to the problem rather than just the problem itself.' Or another useful response. 'If you feel my performance is that bad I'll just leave', with 'I wouldn't want that to happen, I do value X and Y that you add to the team. My aim today is to stop that decision from being taken out of your hands. Let's work together to come up with a plan.'

# Peer feedback

Peer to peer feedback is a game changer for the leader, the individuals, the team and the organisation. We touched upon it in the chapter 'Focus On Yourself First', using the feedback activity from the book *The Five Dysfunctions Of A Team* by Patrick Lencioni. Run this activity at least twice to ensure there is trust throughout the team, then take it to a different level.

The aim here is to get your teams to a point where they expect and are completely comfortable in giving unsolicited feedback to and receiving it from each other. There are very few teams who aspire to reach this level, but when they do, the impact is massive.

As the leader, ask your reports to provide you with feedback. For example, before a team meeting, explain you'd like specific feedback. Give team members a focus point and gratefully accept their feedback. You won't agree with all of it, but demonstrate the bits you accept and will adopt.

Once you have done this a few times, explain that once a week everyone will put themselves in the same position: giving notice of the specific event/meeting and what feedback focus they want. After a few weeks, regroup and hold a meeting to discuss the process and the benefits of the feedback received.

As leader, you can now ask for feedback at any time regarding anything. Ask each person in the team to provide you with one piece of useful feedback in a set period of time. Again, as you're going first, you're not asking them to do anything you're not prepared to do. Once you've had your feedback and can demonstrate how you are incorporating it, require the team to do the same. If the team is large, initially form smaller feedback groups, but each person must accept responsibility for looking for opportunities to give feedback to their peer(s) in a set period of time.

Regroup and discuss. Agree as a group how to embed the practice as the norm, circle back to it often to keep it front of mind and expect progress reports. Once you're sure it's a part of your team's culture, it becomes business as usual.

---

## KEY ENGAGEMENT AUDIT – FEEDBACK

What level of resistance do you have to delivering difficult messages? What resistance do your reports have?

In what ways do you encourage peer feedback in your team? How could you implement the peer feedback process? What impact would that have on team effectiveness and engagement?

How could this be an area of dissatisfaction that causes people to leave your organisation? What can you learn from that?

---

# Massive goals

At this stage, goals that don't leave both you and your team members feeling you may have lost the plot a bit aren't big enough. The goal should come from the team members, with you coaching to ensure it's worthy of them.

---

*If we all did the things we are capable of doing,*

*we would literally astound ourselves.*

**THOMAS EDISON**

---

Let's look at the types of goals people set.

**Type A goals** feel comfortable and represent incremental growth. People know they can achieve them. These goals belong in the **Inspire Self-belief** phase.

**Type B goals** are a stretch and represent the next logical step. People think they could achieve them. These goals belong in the **Educate** phase.

**Type C goals** inspire and scare. People have no idea how they can achieve them, but they really want to. These goals belong in this phase, **Raise The Bar**. Achieving them represents satisfaction, pride and growth.

## Coaching questions

To elicit type C goals and plans, you need to ask provocative, probing questions:

- What one area of your performance is the key to unlocking your potential? What have you done about it?

- How do you ensure you're a top performer? Why is it important to you?

- What assumptions have you made to keep you where you are?

- What assumptions do you think I have about you?

- How do you hold yourself to higher standards than me? In what ways do I need to raise my expectations of you?

- What story are you telling yourself about why you can't achieve X? How has that held you back? How will that hold you back? What will that cost you in the long run?

- If you were going to be twice as effective as you are now, what's the first thing you'd do? Why aren't you doing that already?

- Who are you blaming for your limitations? How can you release them from that obligation?

- If I offered you the role of (add a significant jump), would you take it or hesitate?

Here's a question for you to consider: in what ways are you under delegating? Handing over 'power' and authority is covered in the Empower phase, the final phase of the FIERCE Loyalty® model, but the process begins here.

In addition to massive goals, stretch assignments are a fantastic way to raise the bar significantly. I have found the most useful way to do this is to delegate aspects of my role that are outside the comfort zone of the other person, e.g. chairing global conference calls with senior leaders. There's no real way to prepare for something like that, no trial run to practise. And some of them can be fairly bruising. There's a lot to gain because there's a lot to lose. Something is at stake. It matters.

A great way to identify a real stretch assignment is to look for a task that is usually the responsibility of someone two levels/grades/ranks above the person who will undertake it. It's not a hard and fast rule, but is a good pulse check.

There must be a genuine growth opportunity in the tasks you delegate to your team members. It's not an excuse to offload tedious or time consuming work. Any risk must be carefully assessed and managed. You always retain overall responsibility. People learn by observing, trying, failing, learning, getting better and eventually mastering a task. At some point you have to push the bird out of the nest and hope they fly.

If the delegated experience is positive, then the person's confidence, skill and attitude will take an explosive leap forwards. If the experience is negative, you've got specific things to work on. And although their ego will be bruised, it's not shattered, because you've taken the time to build their self-belief to such a level that it withstands the inevitable knocks.

At this point, people are usually eager and willing to undertake new, challenging assignments. In order to have the most engaging discussions and coaching sessions with them, understand and adapt to their style and preferred way of communication.

Let's use my previous team as an example.

| EMMA - ANALYSER | LISA - INSPIRER | HELEN - HARMONISER | SUE - COMMANDER |
|---|---|---|---|
| **PREFERRED STYLE** | **PREFERRED STYLE** | **PREFERRED STYLE** | **PREFERRED STYLE** |
| ▪ Professional, attention to detail, logical, precise, meets deadlines | ▪ Establishes quick and easy relationships, bubbly, builds trust | ▪ Authentic, humble, takes time to reflect for insight | ▪ Energetic, enthusiastic, creative, lively, has presence |
| **MY COMMUNICATION FOR STRETCH ASSIGNMENTS** | **MY COMMUNICATION FOR STRETCH ASSIGNMENTS** | **MY COMMUNICATION FOR STRETCH ASSIGNMENTS** | **MY COMMUNICATION FOR STRETCH ASSIGNMENTS** |
| ▪ 'I need your attention to detail on xx.' <br> ▪ 'This important project needs someone with your precision.' <br> ▪ 'You're the expert, what's the logical answer?' <br> ▪ 'You can see things from all angles, what's the right approach?' | ▪ 'Help me to create xx.' <br> ▪ 'Your enthusiasm is infectious.' <br> ▪ 'I need to rely on your can-do attitude.' <br> ▪ 'I want to involve you in something big that's going to impact the entire organisation.' <br> ▪ 'I need your intuition on this one.' | ▪ 'I need your support with the team.' <br> ▪ 'This project needs someone who can see other people's perspective.' <br> ▪ 'If I wanted to boost morale, what advice would you give me?' | ▪ 'You're ready for this challenge.' <br> ▪ 'You've had a strong impact.' <br> ▪ 'You're my strongest performer in xx.' <br> ▪ 'I know you'll find a quick solution to xx.' <br> ▪ 'I'd like your ideas about the direction.' |
| **TO DEVELOP THEIR SKILLS AS PART OF THE ASSIGNMENT** | | | |
| ▪ 'During this assignment, I want you to have team impact front of mind as the primary goal.' | ▪ 'During this task, I want you to create specific performance measures/stats and update me daily.' | ▪ 'You need to feedback on areas of the organisation/leader underperformance and make suggestions to improve it.' | ▪ 'I want you to gather everyone's inputs before making your recommendation.' |

People are fiercely loyal when they have passion for what they do and a sense of purpose. They get out of bed in the morning with a spring in their step because they know what they're doing matters, they make a difference, and they're great at it.

People are no longer happy doing joyless, meaningless jobs for leaders who treat them like numbers. Growth as people, not just in a work context, is the new expectation. If you can take people on that journey, you will win the loyalty game. If not, you'll keep on asking, 'Why aren't my people engaged?'

If you get people successfully to this stage, you're in touching distance of the prize: FIERCE Loyalty®. If it hasn't happened already, this is the point where people become role models of excellence.

---

## KEY ENGAGEMENT AUDIT – MASSIVE GOALS

Who in your team is ready for a C-level goal? How will you communicate that to them?

Which of your responsibilities could you delegate as a stretch assignment? To whom?

What's the first two-level assignment or task you could delegate? What's the possible gain? What's the risk?

How could this be an area of dissatisfaction that causes people to leave your organisation? What can you learn from that?

---

# Summary

- Significant gear shifts built on solid self-belief can transform people and their performance

- Give the important tough feedback

- Demand and role model a culture of unsolicited peer feedback

- Help people to set goals that defy logic

- If there's nothing to lose, there's nothing to gain. Stretch assignments that involve a degree of risk catapult people forwards.

# CAREER
# CONVERSATIONS

---

*Train people well enough so they can leave,*
*treat them well enough so they don't want to.*

**RICHARD BRANSON**

---

What if you measured your performance as a leader by the number of internal moves and promotions from your team? What if new members of your team knew from the start that you already had an eye on preparing them for their next move? What if instead of creating followers, you focused on creating more leaders?

CFO: 'What happens if we spend money training our people and then they leave?'

CEO: 'What happens if we don't and they stay?'

Internal moves are not only inevitable, they are essential. This can be a tough stage for leaders. They've spent months or years moulding employees and cultivating skill and performance. It's hard to see them move on; it can even feel disloyal.

It helps at this stage to remind yourself that your commitment is to your organisation, not just your team or division. If you are contributing to the overall success and health of your organisation by developing a pipeline of successors to fill internal vacancies, then feel great about that. Plus, the vacuum left by the outgoing team member creates an opportunity for others in the team who may have been wondering where their career was going.

---

*Leaders don't create followers,*

*they create more leaders.*

**TOM PETERS**

---

This section of the book is relatively short, and like most parts of the model, it is actually surprisingly simple. The issue isn't in the complexity of the information; it's whether leaders are doing it, and doing it at the right time.

Internal moves and promotions need to be encouraged and planned for well in advance. The conversation that prompts the search, if it hasn't already started, begins in the Career Conversations phase of the model, and you initiate it.

During my time with American Express, the company was in *The Times* **Top 100 Employers** for many years running. One of the aspects I admired and appreciated was the company's internal move culture. Tenure overall in the organisation was exceptionally high. We were frequently applauding people for five, ten, even fifteen years or more with the company, so rare these days. But although people stayed in the company, they rarely stayed in the same role or department for more than two years. It wasn't uncommon for leaders at Director level to change departments. The ethos was focused on rich diversity of knowledge learned in role, rather than experience initially bought to the role. It was the same for all levels in the company, and was encouraged. Typically after twelve to eighteen months in a role, the leader would initiate a conversation about a team member's next role, and plans would begin to get the person as ready as possible. It was an incredible culture. Needless to say, engagement was high.

But although we want people to soar when it comes to their career, there needs to be an element of reality. If you genuinely feel their goal is outside of the person's grasp, now is the time to be candid. It rarely happens, as in my experience people are far more likely to downplay their potential, but speak up if needed.

Ask yourself, 'What's my long game?' If your performance as leader was measured on the number of internal moves/promotions, a year from now what would you be doing differently? What would you need to start doing differently today to make that a reality?

How many people would you expect to have left your team for another internal position? Who specifically? How do you know that? What's standing in their way? What are the obvious solutions?

If every person reporting in to you, and their direct reports, took a step forward in the next two years, what would that look like? What's the current biggest obstacle to that happening? How much money would that save the organisation?

If your objective is to have 100% internal turnover in your team in the next two years, how would you make that happen? How would you feel about that? What impact would it have? Who needs to be involved in this discussion?

Are your team's personal development plans up to date? Are they clear and robust? If not, when and how will that happen?

Who will be your successor? Who is the star you haven't identified yet? How can your top performers support the rest of the team?

The GROW coaching model is especially useful for career conversations. Here are a few example questions. If the model is new to you, there is a vast amount of information online.

| GOAL DESIRED FUTURE STATE | REALITY CURRENT STATE | OPTIONS POSSIBILITIES | WILL AND WAY FORWARD SPECIFIC ACTION PLAN |
|---|---|---|---|
| • What's the main goal you're focused on at the moment? <br> • What tells you that's the priority? <br> • What would success look like? <br> • Twelve months from now, what would make you most proud? <br> • What is important to you in your career and day to day experience? <br> • What would keep you committed to the organisation? <br> • What's your dream role? <br> • If you had the experience/skills, what role would you apply for? | • What have you done so far to achieve this? <br> • How effective was that? <br> • What do you feel is standing in your way? <br> • What's stopping you from...? <br> • What difference would this make to you? <br> • What skills do you need? <br> • What assumptions have you made to keep you where you are? <br> • How do you hold yourself to higher standards than me? | • If you were advising me, what advice would you give? <br> • When have you faced a similar situation? <br> • Who could you speak to? <br> • Who is the role model? <br> • What are some of the next steps you can take towards your goal? <br> • What experiences do you need in your present role to prepare you? <br> • How have you engaged existing role holders? | • What's your first step? <br> • What will have the biggest/quickest impact? <br> • By when? <br> • What can you foresee standing in your way? <br> • What can/will you do about it? <br> • How should I hold you accountable for this? <br> • On a scale of 1-10, how committed are you to achieving this? <br> • How will you maintain motivation and engagement in the meantime? |

You began planting the seeds for this element in the Inspire Self-belief phase, where you broadcast your team's achievements to the wider organisation. This is the same principle, but it works at an individual level.

When you become aware that an individual has aspirations to gain a promotion or move to another team, while they are working on what you both agree needs to be undertaken to ready them for the role. you can act as advocate for that individual to a key person or even the decision maker.

There are various ways to achieve this:

- Highlight excellent performance in a conversation
- For a stretch assignment, the key person could delegate a piece of their work, e.g. a report
- As the person successfully gains new knowledge or skills pertinent to the team they wish to join, highlight that success to relevant stakeholders.

The key is to be transparent with the other leader(s). Tell them that your team member has aspirations to join their team and highlight the positive steps they are taking to get there. Organise a meeting with all three of you where together you map out the path to success. The team member will see this as a sign of trust, recognition and respect, and their loyalty will reach an all-time high.

Internal moves are the successful culmination of your efforts as a great leader. But not everyone will want to move. In fact, people can become so fiercely loyal that they stifle their career advancement in order to stay close to their leader. Watch out for and discourage this. As leader, your aim is to help others to reach their full potential, which isn't necessarily in your team. Plus, when you yourself eventually move onwards and upwards, they will have to carry on without you.

Help them to step out of your shadow. At this stage in their development, it's preventing them from growing. Give them the nudges they need to succeed and become great leaders themselves.

## KEY ENGAGEMENT AUDIT – CAREER CONVERSATIONS

Do the development plans for your reports include career aspirations? How frequently do you refer to them and check in on progress?

If you measured yourself and your leader-level reports on internal moves/promotions, what impact would that have on the business? The team? Employees? Engagement? Yourself? What would need to happen for this to become a reality? Is your organisation ready for that? Are you ready for that?

When was the last time you intentionally advocated for someone in your team to move internally? What opportunities do you have to increase your advocacy?

How could this be an area of dissatisfaction that causes people to leave your organisation? What can you learn from that?

# Summary

- Internal movers from your team should be the expected norm

- Create the expectation early on that people will move

- Elicit the specific career move from the other person. You can only guide

- Advocate to other leaders in your organisation

- Don't allow the person's loyalty to you as the leader to stifle their career advancement. Create leaders, not followers.

# EMPOWER

---

*A leader is best when people barely
know he exists, when his work is done, his aim
fulfilled, they will say: we did it ourselves.*

**LAO TZU**

---

What if your people had unlocked so much of their own talent that they no longer needed to be led? What if your working relationship switched tracks to one where you were a trusted business advisor? What if you could stop issuing instructions in all but the most serious crises or risky situations?

You've made it. You have learned how to inspire, engage, support and lead your reports successfully to release their full potential and demand more of themselves than they ever have before. Take a breath here. Think about that for a moment. The positive ripple-effects you can create in people's lives are astonishing. The path they run on will affect the quality of their lives, the richness of their relationships with others, the height of the aspirations they have for themselves and their capacity to fulfil them for ever. I know - I frequently think about Brigid and can see the fingerprints of her leadership in my own.

So what now?

Now is the time to take a big step back. Your team should be setting massive goals, forging new relationships and networks, delivering with excellence. Basically, they should be leading themselves.

You've achieved what so many leaders and organisations aspire to, but sadly don't reach - success through the will of the people. And there you have it, why employee engagement is so important: anything meaningful that you want to achieve in your business can only translate into operational reality and succeed in the long run with the will of the people, and that is only achieved through engagement.

---

*When we give our people more authority, we actually create more effective leaders.*

**DAVID MARQUET**

---

In the chapter 'Inspire Self-belief', I made reference to the book *Turn the Ship Around* by David Marquet. It's brilliant, a must read. In a bid to turn around the performance on the nuclear submarine he commanded, he stopped giving orders altogether (he did retain sole responsibility for the command to launch a nuclear strike). Instead, he guided self-discovered solutions through a series of questions to satisfy himself that the other person had considered any risk or relevant factors and was anticipating potential challenges.

In my world with my team, this might look something like:

| WHAT I WANT TO TELL THEM TO DO | WHAT I ASK INSTEAD FOR OWNERSHIP, CLEAR THINKING AND SOLID SOLUTION |
|---|---|
| Don't forget to include the HR Director in the outgoing communications. | ▪ What's the risk if we only communicate up to this level?<br>▪ Who is the ultimate stakeholder? |
| XX isn't the right person to authorise the budget | ▪ Who signed off the previous roll out of this programme?<br>▪ As things stand, what's the biggest risk?<br>▪ Financially, who owns this part of the project? |
| That's not the global priority. The regional delivery will have to happen Q2. | ▪ Talk me through the thinking behind making this your priority.<br>▪ If xxx happened, who would be impacted?<br>▪ How can we have the biggest organisational impact this quarter?<br>▪ What are the pros and cons of making this a priority over the global project? |
| Review the engagement scores before you start work on the programme design. | ▪ What data will you need to validate the request for this programme?<br>▪ What's the source data for this request?<br>▪ How can we demonstrate we've included the voice of the employees in this programme design? |
| We should be focusing on XX. | ▪ How are we playing it small with this approach? |

Once I'm happy the team member has a solid solution based on clear thinking (and often their solutions are better than my own), I let them carry on. Sometimes I request an update, depending on the task; sometimes I don't.

This is still a worrying thought for most leaders, though.

I came across this gem recently: a list of what leaders worry about. Seems like only 4% is legitimate and controllable.

- 40% worry about things that never happen (the company really won't fold if the task you're handing over fails)

- 30% worry about things in the past (the person has come a long way since X happened)

- 12% worry about needless health concerns

- 10% worry about insignificant, petty worries (often personality rather than task based)

- 8% worry about legitimate concerns - 4% that can be controlled, 4% that cannot.

Don't let your fears and anxiety prevent this final part of the transformation of your teams. Be alert, just don't let it hold you or your team back.

In the chapter 'Raise The Bar', we touched upon delegation. I want to circle back to it here. When to delegate and how to delegate come into full effect in the Empower phase.

Let's consider how to delegate.

**Start with the end in mind.** Get crystal clear about the desired outcome, deadlines, checkpoints and measures of success.

**Set clear boundaries.** This may include financial limits. What specifically is the person responsible for? If limits of authority are being reached, should the person:

- Wait to be told what to do?

- Ask what to do?

- Make recommendations? Within what timescales?

- Act, and then report results immediately?

- Initiate action, and then report out?

**Try to match responsibility with authority.** This may mean increasing authority levels. The person needs the chance to make some decisions, even if that means the risk of failing, but remember, ultimately the buck stops with you.

**Provide adequate support without taking over.**

**Provide necessary resources.**

**Focus on the outcome:** what is accomplished, rather than how the work should be done. Chances are their way is better than yours (remember, you're the air traffic controller, not the pilot). Allowing the person to control their own methods, the 'how', shows trust and respect.

**Don't micro-manage.** Remember we learn by observing, trying, failing, learning, getting better and eventually mastering. If you catch people every time they're about to fall, they won't learn.

**Make it OK to fail.** If you've built in robust checks and measures, no failure should be a calamity or massive business risk. In the wise words of Amazon, 'Fail, fail fast and learn'.

**Celebrate and highlight success.**

The Leader as Teacher (LaT) methodology is highly effective within teams, and especially useful when your reports get to this stage of the model. It is a programme that supports leaders within the business to deliver development and learning initiatives. The scale and complexity of the programme may involve a train the trainer programme (T3).

T3 preparation could include:

- Providing leader briefing packs and discussion guidance notes
- Attending the programme as a participant
- Co-facilitating elements of the programme with learning and development colleagues
- Formal observation and sign off from the learning and development function.

The benefits of this approach are numerous:

- Development for the leader (not only in presentation and communication skills, but a deeper understanding of the topic itself)
- Greater self-awareness
- Credibility - people love to hear from their leaders. It adds that 'real world' element to the learning as the leaders draw on examples and experience to bring the subject to life
- Greater reach - there are only so many people in the learning and development function, limiting the number of programmes that can be supported
- Exposing leaders to a wider range of employees and ideas
- Freeing learning and development up to innovate new programmes
- Strengthening the culture of communication and transparency
- Engaging and stimulating by providing variety.

Not only do you teach, but the talent you've developed to this point does as well. This can be in the form of mentoring, coaching, LaT or all three, but they are expected to support the rest of the team.

If you're constantly looking over the shoulders of employees, you're little more than a babysitter. Get your teams to want to stretch out on their own and lead others. If they fail, they'll have learned a lot in the process and gained the respect of their colleagues. They will also be preparing themselves to be great empowering leaders of the future.

I've often heard people say that they have no idea what their boss does. Even busy and effective leaders can quickly lose respect if there isn't transparency and openness about the role they play.

This presents an opportunity. The chances are, most of your employees aren't used to thinking at the executive level, since they're busy with their own tasks and roles. However, to develop them for upward moves into more senior roles, help them see the bigger picture and consider things from a higher vantage point. This benefits everyone.

In team meetings, share with them the strategic plans and projects within your organisation. Help your team understand the main goals that you're driving towards. Give them an overview on how other divisions are performing – the more pieces of the puzzle your team gains, the easier it will be for them to enter the executive mindset.

## KEY ENGAGEMENT AUDIT – EMPOWER

If you stopped issuing instructions, which would you have to retain responsibility for? Which instructions could you stop giving now?

How could you implement a Leader as Teacher programme in your team? What opportunities exist to develop the senior leader mindset?

How could this be an area of dissatisfaction that causes people to leave your organisation? What can you learn from that?

# Summary

- Don't issue orders, ask smart questions

- Delegate, don't abdicate

- Adopt the Leader as Teacher methodology for yourself and your top talent.

# CONCLUSION

*If I have seen further it is by standing
on the shoulders of giants.*

**ISAAC NEWTON**

Once you have led your team to this point, they should be highly engaged and fiercely loyal. It's not hard; it's not beyond anyone's reach. In fact, it's blindingly simple if you want it and you're prepared to change the way you view and approach being a leader. You don't even need to make big changes, just the right changes.

**Aware.** As the leader, you'll be amazed how much weight your actions and opinions carry. Your approval, attention and direction carry weight. Your unguarded unconstructive comments demotivate. Everything you do is magnified. Small things to you are big things to others. But if this has been holding you back, the great news is it's also the mechanism by which you can improve, easily.

**Care.** There has never been a greater need for transformational leaders. The people you influence reflect and radiate the way you make them feel far beyond the workplace, to their families, friends and associates.

You have a unique opportunity to be an incredible role model; an example of how to conduct yourself with poise in the face of challenges. In being fair and consistent and treating others with respect, even when they mess up, you make lifelong learning, growth and excellence the yardstick by which they measure themselves and their contribution.

Imagine a society where every person had such a positive role model, teacher and mentor.

**Dare.** What are you prepared to give up to achieve this? Or start? Or get even better at? How, as the leader, will you show you're going first so that others want to follow? How will you face into the difficult challenges and stay the course until new ways of behaving and a new culture emerge?

**Share.** How will you involve your peers, stakeholders and the wider organisation? How will you convince them to join you? Once you've mastered this with your team, how will you showcase and freely share the learnings with other leaders? How will you get this adopted in your organisation?

**Partnership.** Understanding the ideas presented in this book isn't going to challenge you. The adoption and implementation, where the transformation happens, is usually where leaders and organisations need support.

Leading Edge Performance specialises in the implementation of these ideas. If you want an initial indication of how your leadership style supports engagement, try our free online scorecard at www.LeadingEdgePerformace.org/scorecard. You can also download our free report '7 Mistakes Most Leaders Make' and our cost of attrition report 'The Silent Profit Killer' at www.LeadingEdgePerformace.org/publications.

If you want to take the next step and discuss the results, or where your organisation currently is and how to take massive steps forward, with one of our engagement specialists, please call us on 07547 532528 or email info@LeadingEdgePerformance.org to book a discovery session.

# Acknowledgements

The quote from Isaac Newton that introduces the Conclusion to this book barely begins to cover the debt of gratitude I owe to the magnificent leaders and inspirational peers I've worked with over the years. To call out a few from many:

**Brigid Slevin**, you showed me a new way to be that went far beyond my job. I have been the light to so many people since we worked together, and I lit my candle from yours. Thank you.

**Paul Simpson**, you taught me that tough leaders command respect and create followers. You also role modelled persistence to me, a quality I'm constantly working on.

**Michele McNickle Driver**, I always loved your straight talking. You taught me about having good intentions and assuming others do too. You're also the best hostess ever!

**Stephanie Seracka**, you showed me the true power of collaboration and how two minds bent on the same outcome can create and innovate far beyond the abilities of either one. And your attention to detail is mind-blowing.

**Graham Truluck**, you had the greatest capacity to be curious and coach in the moment I have ever encountered. You also always had a clear desk, which taught me that overt activity and leadership effectiveness aren't the same thing.

**Sue Clark**, you allowed me to feel the warmth of positive reinforcement and the fear of massive stretch assignments, giving me the space and belief to make quantum leaps in performance.

**Andre Marcos**, you embody a quality I admire highly: you believe and act upon the idea that the success of others elevates us all. You are the first and loudest voice in support of other people's wins.

**Nuala Murphy and Tim Hewitt**, I'm eternally grateful for your wisdom and support in shaping the final version of this book. I would not have sought counsel from or placed my leadership heart and soul into the hands of anyone else.

# The Author

Louise is a speaker, author and thought leader on numerous topics related to leadership capability and driving employee engagement.

She founded Leading Edge Performance in 2016 after a twenty-five year corporate career in Learning & Development. She draws her experience as much from her years as a leadership development expert as from being a successful leader.

She has worked with hundreds of leaders in dozens of leadership teams all over the world, from global giants such as Amazon and American Express, to UK financial services and utilities companies. Her goal is to give leaders the tools and ambition to create stimulating and engaging workplaces where people grow and thrive.

In 2004, Louise took a sabbatical to travel around the world. Along the way, she not only met a wide array of fascinating people, she had the privilege of experiencing the richness of cultures such as Thailand, Cambodia, Peru and Guatemala. She taught English on the Honduran Island of Roatan in 2006 before moving to Thailand to run her own scuba diving business. She returned to UK at the end of 2008.

She lives and breathes personal excellence and regularly contributes articles to LinkedIn. She volunteers for the charity Age UK, dedicating time to spend with older people in her local community to offer companionship and mental stimulation.

You can find out more about, and contact, Louise at:
www.louisemallam.com

Facebok - Leading Edge Performance
Twitter - Louise_Mallam
Linkedin - Louise Mallam

Lightning Source UK Ltd.
Milton Keynes UK
UKOW05f1405280417

300121UK00008B/183/P